Robert Kissick

A philosophical history of the formation of the American republic

From its beginning to the end of the civil war

Robert Kissick

A philosophical history of the formation of the American republic
From its beginning to the end of the civil war

ISBN/EAN: 9783337224851

Printed in Europe, USA, Canada, Australia, Japan

Cover: Foto ©ninafisch / pixelio.de

More available books at **www.hansebooks.com**

A PHILOSOPHICAL HISTORY

OF THE

FORMATION

OF THE

AMERICAN REPUBLIC

From Its Beginning to the End
of the Civil War.

BY

ROBT. KISSICK, LL. B.

OF THE

OSKALOOSA, IOWA, BAR.

To

MY WIFE

Whose suggestions and criticisms have been of great

benefit to me in the preparation

of this work,

THIS VOLUME

Is affectionately dedicated.

A PHILOSOPHICAL HISTORY

OF

THE FORMATION

OF

THE AMERICAN REPUBLIC.

CONTENTS.

BOOK I.

A Philosophical View of the Formation and Evolution
of the Republic.

PART I.

The Origin, Necessity and Object of Government—The
Causes that Led to the Formation of our Republic—
The Steps Taken in Its Formation, with Some Results
Consequent on the Manner of Its Formation.

CHAPTER I.

CHAPTER II.

CHAPTER III.

CHAPTER IV.

CHAPTER V.

PART II.

Two Civilizations—Their Rise and Development—The
Fall of One and the Triumph of the Other.

CHAPTER I.

CHAPTER II.

CHAPTER III.

CHAPTER IV.

CHAPTER V.

CHAPTER VI.

CHAPTER VII.

CHAPTER VIII.

CHAPTER IX.

CHAPTER X.

CHAPTER XI.

TO THE PEOPLE OF THE UNITED STATES.

"One-half of the time which is now almost wasted, in district schools, on English grammar, attempted at too early an age, would be sufficient to teach our children to love the Republic, and to become its loyal and life-long supporters. After the bloody baptism from which the Nation has arisen to a higher and nobler life, if this shameful defect in our system of education be not speedily remedied, we shall deserve the infinite contempt of future generations. I insist that it should be made an indispensable condition of graduation in every American college, that the student must understand the history of this continent since its discovery by Europeans, the origin and history of the United States, its constitution of government, the struggles through which it has passed, and the rights and duties of citizens who are to determine its destiny and share its glory."—James A. Garfield, in 1867.

PREFACE.

It may be thought that the scope of my work is too narrow; or, in other words, that I have not used all the events which go to make up the formation and evolution of the Republic. From one point of view this is true, to some extent. This work, however, has been written on the theory that our Republic was evolved, and has been perpetuated, out of conflicts between freedom and tyranny; that its philosophy rests upon the principle that all men are created equal, as expressed in the great Declaration. So long as inalienable rights were denied, to some or all of the people, conflicts were certain to take place, to right the wrong. Indeed, the history of the past two or three centuries or more consists largely of a series of struggles for freedom. What battles have been fought, what millions have died for the rights of man! Tyranny became intrenched in power, and would not let go; so Freedom had to battle for her rights. Freedom, though "scarred" with her many wars, by these has added strength to strength, to meet her ever vigilant and sleepless enemy in combat—finally to be victorious. Thus it ever has been; thus it ever will be. In this way freedom progresses, and civilization rises to a higher plane.

With the thought that freedom is the pole star
—the central idea—of our Republic, around which
clings all else, I have confined myself to an outline
of the great struggles between freedom and tyranny, in giving a philosophical view of its formation and evolution. I have tried to deal only with
fundamentals, leaving details to be looked for else-
where.

The great drama of history naturally divides
itself into periods; and generally there is a central idea or principle in each from which it must
be viewed when treating it philosophically.

It may be truly said that the three greatest
periods in the history of the world, since the beginning of the Christian era, are, the discovery of
a New World, by Columbus; the founding of a
nation, by Washington; and the preservation of
that nation, by Lincoln. These are the ones which
have had, and which will still have, the greatest
influence on humanity for its betterment. There
is nothing mythical about these periods. Able
writers have written of them, and none need be
ignorant of their history. He, who will, may read
and understand.

It has been my endeavor, in this volume, to
give a faithful exposition of the leading events of
the second and third periods; they have been my
theme; their history the warp and woof of my
story.

What grander theme than the founding of a nation—a Republic—at the time, and under the circumstances, in which it was founded; and the

preservation of that Republic—after it had grown
mighty among the nations of the world—from its
internal foes! The history of these events should
be familiar to all its people; and especially to the
boys and girls—for in them is the future hope of
the Republic.

Patriotism, — love of country, — should be
taught in the home, the school, the church, and
to every citizen of the Republic. If this be done
better citizens will be the result, and in consequence better government. Too many know but
little, if anything, of the history of the formation
of our Republic, of what it cost to build it, and
the great cost of its maintenance.

In what way can patriotism be better taught
than by giving a knowledge of the fundamental
principles of liberty, of our government, and of
what it cost to build and maintain the Republic?
These I have tried to set forth in the spirit of the
philosophy of the great events which have transpired in its building from its infancy up to the
close of the war for the preservation of the Union.
And, in doing this, I have given the landmarks
which were made in its evolution during that
time. Some of them fell by the wayside in that
evolution; but all that were worthy of preservation still endure, and it is hoped will endure forever; for they are founded on right, the only sure
and stable foundation of government.

Those landmarks which have stood the test of
time, and the shock of battle, have been established in blood. They should be sacred to the peo-

ple and nourished by them with patriotic devo-
tion. I have set forth the landmarks which have
survived and those which have perished, that each
may judge for himself whether the right or the
wrong survived, in the great conflicts through
which the Republic has passed. I have attempted
to inform the student as to fundamental principles, and thus to assist in guiding him in his
search after the truth of what was the right, or
the wrong, of those conflicts; and in doing that I
have sought to do so in a spirit of fairness and
impartiality to all. Whether or not I have succeeded, in this, I submit to the judgment of the
reader.

If this book inspires in the reader a love of
truth, of country, of right, and a hatred of wrong,
I shall feel that my labors have not been in vain.

It has been a conviction of mine for years, that
the study of the history of the formation of the
Republic has been and is too much neglected. It
may be that some of the facts are pretty thoroughly taught to the young, but I am led to believe
that the philosophy of the real facts has been
greatly neglected, as well as the fundamental principles of liberty and of our government; and this
to the prejudice of good government.

The naked facts of history are said to be dry
and uninteresting. This, to some extent, is true;
and, unless they are imbued with a soul, but little
interest will be taken in them by the average student.

History—pure or scientific history—should be

written and studied the same as any other branch of knowledge requiring the use of the reasoning powers. The reason of things should be clearly brought before the mind. If this be done the mind of the student will the more readily grasp the relevancy or relation of events; without this he is groping, as it were, in the darkness, not knowing whither he is going or where he will land. In this way only will its study bear fruit worthy the human mind.

The foundation principles of the Republic rest upon the Declaration of Independence; and this, with the Constitution of the United States, constitutes the Great Charter of our liberties; the Constitution being the organic and fundamental law of the land. These great instruments should be the study of all. Their language,—together with the history of their formation, and the causes which inspired and led to their adoption,—should be well known. "He can but poorly appreciate the freedom he enjoys," says an eminent jurist, "who does not understand the great charter which secures it. I was about to go further, and say, that he does not deserve to be free, who will not inform himself in what his freedom consists."

The study of these instruments should not be confined to any one class. Persons of all occupations and professions should be familiar with them and their history. But especially should the youth of the land be required to learn their text by heart, as were the Roman youth the law of the "twelve tables." If this were done citizenship would be

higher, and the perpetuity of the Government,—of
the people, by the people, and for the people,—be
better assured and rest on a firmer and more enduring basis.

In addition to these all should carefully study
the utterances of Washington and Lincoln. Had
their wisdom and counsels prevailed, in the hearts
of their countrymen, this land would not have
been drenched in fraternal blood. Their words
are applicable to all times; and at the present
time their patriotic sayings should be treasured
in the minds of all, for a new era is dawning in
the Republic. If this Republic ever goes down it
will be from its internal foes, and not those without. Let all take heed to the eloquent and faithful
words of its Founder and its Preserver,—then its
future will be well assured.

In this history I have drawn the curtain at
the close of the War for the Union; not because
what lies beyond is devoid of interest, for it is of
great interest, but because the events which have
transpired since, are too near to us to be viewed
in the light of impartial history,—the point of
view is not distant enough. The sediment of the
events has not yet settled so as to leave the real
facts transparent enough to write of them in the
light of a clear perception of their real character,
and their relation to the welfare of the Republic.

The author has designed this book as an
authority in American literature, for use in the
schools and homes of America.

It is submitted, without any apologies, to a

critical public for its perusal, with the hope that
it may inspire, in all, a love for our free institutions, our country, and those who so nobly performed their part in making it what it is,—the
freest, the greatest, the grandest Republic the
world has ever known.

ROBT. KISSICK.

Oskaloosa, Iowa, U. S. A.

July 4th, 1896.

INTRODUCTION.

I have undertaken the task of writing a History of the Formation of our Republic; not by giving an account of its battles, sieges, the early settlement of the country, the development of the colonies, and such like; others have written of these. But I intend, instead thereof, to use the facts of history, and from them write a Philosophical History; giving, in as brief a space as possible, the reason or philosophy of the leading events which have transpired in the building or evolution of the Republic, from its beginning, up to the end of the Great Rebellion in 1865.

I shall endeavor to set forth the great landmarks, the steps she has taken to attain her high state of civilization, and high standing among the civilized nations of the world. For the true test of the progress of a people is their advancement in civilization. Progress is the fruit of knowledge; knowledge the base and regulator of civilization.

I know of no history of the kind; and I have been led to believe that such a history would be one in which the American people would be interested. If it shall prove acceptable to the reader, as I trust it may, I will feel amply repaid for my labors.

The history of a great Republic, like ours,—

19

which has no parallel in the history of nations,
ancient or modern,—should stand first in the affec-
tions of its people, and should be the study of all
its people. Its true greatness and its beneficence
cannot be appreciated unless its people understand the history of its formation, and are willing
to devote their attention to the study of the trials
and vicissitudes through which it passed in its
infancy, and those which have followed. Indeed,
no one can learn of these without having his mind
filled with a love for her priceless institutions,
and for the freedom which all enjoy by reason of
the sacrifices made by those who engaged in the
great conflicts, which have produced such a benefi-
cent result.

The study of history should form a large part
of an education; for, I cannot conceive that one
is well educated unless he is thoroughly versed in
history. · From history we derive our knowledge
of man in his several relations with society; and
as connected with the rise, progress, and decay
of states and nations, in art, science, politics, religion, and all those things which tend either to
promote the happiness or the misery of the people.

Man makes history. · And since history deals
with the actions of men, it is necessary, in writing
history, to look into the causes and motives which
impel men to act in a particular way. For there
is a cause for every effect; and men do not act
without a motive.

It may be said that there are two kinds of
history. One, wherein events are simply narrated,

which may be called "fact history"; the other, wherein the facts of history are so used as to show the reason of the happening of events; that kind may be termed "spirit or soul history."

The second kind of history I believe to be the more useful and important to mankind. For if we do not understand the reason or philosophy of a thing, it cannot be said that we have been much, if any, benefited by its study.

The first kind of history is the storehouse of facts; and, as it were, constitutes the anatomy of history. This anatomy, however, must have life breathed into it, or remain dead to mankind. The true historian, then, will so select, arrange, and use facts, deduce causes, motives, principles, as to give that life. In this way giving to the world the warnings and instructions of history, for which it is chiefly valuable.

It has been said, that history is philosophy teaching by examples. But, I apprehend, the examples will amount to but little unless they are so used as to exemplify the philosophy of events. Its philosophy is the soul of history; and if the soul be not developed it is like the "barren fig tree,"—fruitless.

My effort will be to delineate the soul of our Republic,—Freedom; or, as it were, to paint a picture of its evolution with the facts of history as its background.

PRELUDE.

AMERICA.

My country! 'tis of thee,
Sweet land of liberty,
    Of thee I sing;
Land where my fathers died;
Land of the pilgrim's pride;
From every mountain side,
    Let freedom ring.

My native country! thee,
Land of the noble free,
    Thy name I love;
I love thy rocks and rills,
Thy woods and templed hills;
My heart with rapture thrills,
    Like that above.

Let music swell the breeze,
And ring from all the trees
    Sweet freedom's song;
Let mortal tongues awake,
Let all that breathe partake,
Let rocks their silence break,
    The sound prolong.

Our father's God! to Thee,
Author of liberty!
    To Thee we sing;
Long may our land be bright
With freedom's holy light,
Protect us by Thy might,
    Great God, our King.

BOOK I.

A Philosophical View of the Formation and Evolution of the Republic.

PART I.

THE ORIGIN, NECESSITY AND OBJECT OF GOVERNMENT—
THE CAUSES THAT LED TO THE FORMATION OF OUR
REPUBLIC¹—THE STEPS TAKEN IN ITS FORMATION,
WITH SOME RESULTS CONSEQUENT ON THE MANNER
OF ITS FORMATION.

CHAPTER I.

FUNDAMENTAL PRINCIPLES AND THE ORIGIN OF OUR
REPUBLIC.

Freedom is the original and normal condition of man. All men are born with certain natural rights; and when they dwell together,—with no human laws to restrain and regulate their conduct,—they have complete natural freedom and personal independence, and are governed only by the laws of nature or the moral law, in their relations with one another. In this condition there is a perfect equality of rights and obligations between them. But this is the only equality that exists, for no two persons are, in point of fact, equal either socially, morally, physically or intellectually. An equality of rights and obligations, therefore, is the only equality that can exist among men, either in a state of nature or under civil government.

It is self-evident from the nature of man, and, besides, experience has demonstrated, that when men dwell in communities,—as is natural for them to do, for man is a social being and cannot live alone,—something more than the law of nature is

¹For specified causes, see Declaration of Independence, Chapter 2 of Book II.

needed to preserve harmony and order among them; something more than moral restraint is necessary to protect the rights of each individual, and of all. It is not in the province of man to enforce the laws of nature or the moral law. He has no power to do so; that power belongs to God alone; hence, civil law—human law—is necessary; so that when one tramples on the rights of another there may be a remedy to redress the wrong or enforce the right. Laws are necessary to hinder the strong from oppressing the weak; to prevent might from trampling upon right and establishing the wrong. In short, laws are necessary to enforce and maintain equal and exact justice when justice is denied. But these laws, to be permanent, must be founded on the "higher law."

These considerations being true, it follows that government is necessary to make and enforce such laws as may be for the good of all; otherwise anarchy would prevail and each would be a law unto himself, subject only to the moral law which is not enforceable by man, but only by his Creator.

Two questions arise here. What kind of a government should that be? and how should it be established? It would seem, from the nature of the rights of man, that government should be established by the consent of the governed, and in such form as shall best secure and promote the welfare and happiness of the people to be affected by it. The whole community should have the right to speak on that subject.

If the few strong of a community, seeking power, should establish a government without the consent and against the will of the weak, that would be a government by coercion, and, therefore, despotic. Government established in this way is not sure and stable, as has been shown by experience; for power exercised by the few inevitably leads to tyranny. The people become restive under such a government, and sometime they will seize the opportunity to throw it off and establish another.

Where all have a voice in framing the government none can complain, for that would be a free government, since it would derive all its powers from the consent of the governed; such, for example, is the government of the United States of America, which was erected by the "free voice and joint will" of the people, for their common defense, general welfare, and to secure the blessings of liberty.

From these preliminary considerations it will be readily seen, that the object of government is, and should be, to promote the welfare and happiness of the people—all the people. Justice to all is the end of government. Indeed, it is the end of civil society.

That some governments have not attained this end may justly be attributed, to some extent, to their form, and somewhat to the character of their rulers.

The time will come,—long distant, perhaps,— when all governments will rule with equity, and with the sole end of promoting the happiness and well being of the people.

Great improvement in that direction has been made during the past century or more, and especially since the Republic of the United States has come into existence. The crowned rulers of the Old World have taken lessons of the new Republic, founded in the New World, and based on the principle, "that all men are created equal"; and that governments derive "their just powers from the consent of the governed; that, whenever any form of government becomes destructive of these ends, it is the right of the people to alter or abolish it, and to institute a new government, laying its foundations on such principles, and organizing its powers in such form, as to them shall seem most likely to effect their safety and happiness."[2]

When that grand declaration was made by the fathers of the Republic, the rulers of the Old World heard the announcement with bated breath and with astonishment. No such doctrine had ever been announced before. But it was in accordance with the sublime teachings of Him who spake as never man spake. The claimed "divine right" of kings was becoming a myth; and man was asserting his right to self government.

Its promulgation has had the effect to modify the harshness of the governments of the Old World; and the people by reason of it have enjoyed more liberty than ever before. It should be

[2]See Declaration of Independence, Chapter 2 of Book II.

placed, in letters of gold, on the throne of every
crowned head of the nations of the world.

That declaration was the result of long continued tyranny and oppression on the part of the
English Crown, over the people of her Colonies
in America. It was wrung from them when all
hope of redress, for wrongs, had fled; and when
they must either assert their rights as freemen or
become slaves to a tyrant. And thus out of tyranny and oppression was born a new Republic,
where liberty should be inspired with hope, and
which should become the wonder of the nations
of the earth.

Nowhere but in the New World could such a
republic have been erected. Here all was new.
The very air was fatal to the arbitrary institutions of the Old World. Here man was not con-
taminated with the restrained freedom of the
effete institutions of the Old World. He breathed
the air of freedom in his roamings through the
forests, over the hills and mountains of the New.
All around him was wild and free; and his soul
revolted against tyranny and oppression.

He was engaged in a conflict with nature, on
the one side, for his sustenance and physical well
being; and on the other side he was engaged in
battling with the forces of oppression against his
rights as a freemen,—the rights the God of nature
had given him. The living principle of freedom
was implanted within him, and when tyranny and
oppression became unendurable to him as a free-
man, he asserted his rights and independence.

In this way the time came when the colonists of America asserted their rights, threw off the yoke of the English oppressor, and made the declaration "that all men are created equal; and are endowed by their Creator with certain inalienable rights; that among these are life, liberty and the pursuit of happiness."[3]

This declaration, and their independence, they maintained by the sword. From Lexington to Yorktown the patriots of the Revolution,—with Washington[4] as their leader,—contended for seven long years, with a heroism unparalleled, for the rights of man. At Yorktown the forces of oppression surrendered to the forces of liberty, and their heroic efforts were crowned with success. Washington and his compatriots then laid down their arms, and returned to their homes, to help build a nation, freed from the oppressions of their former master. In this, Washington was the guide, —the leader,—as he had been through the war. All eyes were turned to him in the great work of building the new Republic.

---

[3]See Declaration of Independence, Chapter 2 of Book II.

[4]George Washington, Commander-in-Chief of the patriot army during the Revolution, was born at Bridges Creek, Virginia, on the Potomac, about fifty miles south of where Washington now stands. His father, soon after the birth of George, removed to an estate on the Rappahannock opposite Fredericksburg. Washington's great-grandfather, John Washington, emigrated from England to Virginia about 1657. It is generally thought that he belonged to one of the old Cavalier families that fought in behalf of Charles I during the English Civil War. George Washington received a fair English education, but nothing more. He early excelled in athletic sports, horsemanship and as a soldier during the Colonial Wars; these prepared him for his future great work. By the death of his brother, Lawrence Washington, he came eventually into possession of the estate of Mount Vernon, on the Potomac, a short distance below the present city of Washington. In 1759 he married Mrs. Martha Custis, a wealthy widow. From this time on until his death, December 14, 1799, he stood the most prominent of any of the patriots of the Revolution or, indeed, of any in the world. Washington will always be known as the "Father of his Country."

What a grand spectacle was here presented! None such had ever been shown to the world before.

Their success in that great struggle for liberty and independence had a deeper and broader meaning, and the result was of more significance, than simply the independence of the Colonies from the English Crown.

Not only was the yoke of tyranny and oppression thrown off and liberty maintained in America, but the success of the Americans preserved the liberties of the people of England.

An eminent English historian[5] says of that Revolution, and its influence on the liberties of England:

"On the other side of the Atlantic, a great people, provoked by the intolerable injustice of the English government, rose in arms, turned on their oppressors, and, after a desperate struggle, gloriously obtained their independence. In 1776, the Americans laid before Europe that noble Declaration, which ought to be hung up in the nursery of every king, and blazoned on the porch of every royal palace. In words, the memory of which can never die, they declared, that the object of the institution of government is to secure the rights of the people; that from the people alone it derives its powers; and that whenever any form of government becomes destructive of these ends, it is the right of the people to alter or abolish it, and to institute a new government, laying its

---

[5]Buckle, "History of Civilization in England."

3

foundations on such principles, and organizing its powers in such form, as to them shall seem most likely to effect their safety and happiness.

"In order to enforce the monstrous claim of taxing a whole people without their consent, there was waged against America a war ill-conducted, unsuccessful, and what is far worse, accompanied by cruelties disgraceful to a civilized nation. To this may be added, that an immense trade was nearly annihilated; every branch of commerce was thrown into confusion; we were disgraced in the eyes of Europe; we incurred an expense of £140,-000,000; and we lost by far the most valuable colonies any nation has ever possessed.

"Such were the first fruits of the policy of George III.[6] But the mischief did not stop there. The opinions which it was necessary to advocate in order to justify this barbarous war, recoiled on ourselves. In order to defend the attempt to destroy the liberties of America, principles were laid down which, if carried into effect, would have subverted the liberties of England. Not only in the court, but in both houses of Parliament, from the Episcopal bench, and from the pulpits of the church party, there were promulgated doctrines of the most dangerous kind,—doctrines unsuited to a limited monarchy, and, indeed, incompatible with it. The extent to which this reaction proceeded is known to but few readers, because the evidence of it is chiefly to be found in the parliamentary debates, and in the theological litera-

---

⁶King of England.

ture, particularly the sermons, of that time, none
of which are now much studied. But, not to anti-
cipate matters belonging to another part of this
work, it is enough to say, that the danger was
so imminent as to make the ablest defenders of
popular liberty believe that everything was at
stake; and that if the Americans were vanquished,
the next step would be to attack the liberties of
England, and endeavour to extend to the mother
country the same arbitrary government which by
that time would have been established in the Colonies.

"Whether or not these fears were exaggerated,
is a question of considerable difficulty; but after
a careful study of that time, and a study, too, from
sources not much used by historians, I feel satis-
fied that they who are best acquainted with the
period will be the most willing to admit that,
though the danger may have been overrated, it
was far more serious than men are now inclined
to believe. At all events, it is certain that the
general aspect of political affairs was calculated
to excite great alarm. It is certain that, during
many years, the authority of the crown continued
to increase, until it reached a height of which no
example had been seen in England for several
generations. It is certain that the Church of England exerted all her influence in favour of those
despotic principles which the king wished to enforce. It is also certain that, by the constant
creation of new peers, all holding the same views,
the character of the House of Lords was under-

going a slow but decisive change; and that, whenever a favourable opportunity arose, high judicial
appointments were conferred upon men notorious
for their leaning towards the royal prerogative.
These are facts which cannot be denied; and putting them together, there remains, I think, no
doubt, that the American war was a great crisis
in the history of England, and that if the Colonists
had been defeated, our liberties would have been
for a time in considerable jeopardy. From that
risk we were saved by the Americans, who with
heroic spirit resisted the royal armies, defeated
them at every point, and at length, separating
themselves from the mother country, began that
wonderful career, which in less than eighty years
has raised them to an unexampled prosperity, and
which to us ought to be deeply interesting, as
showing what may be effected by the unaided
resources of a free people."

CHAPTER II.

WASHINGTON AND THE CONFEDERATION.

A sense of imminent and common danger, had
caused the Colonies to unite, at the beginning of
the Revolutionary struggle, and to intrust their
interests to a Congress,—composed of delegates
from each Colony,—called the Continental Congress. The delegates to that Congress were instructed, in general terms, to take care of the

liberties of the country. This they did. But it soon became evident that a formal instrument should be adopted, defining with precision, the nature and powers of the union.

While the Declaration of Independence was under consideration in that Congress, in June, 1776, measures were taken by it for the establish-, ment of a constitutional form of government. But nothing was agreed upon until the 15th of November, 1777; on which day, "Articles of Confederation and Perpetual Union" were adopted by the Congress.[7] When these articles were sent by Congress to the State legislatures for their ratification, they were declared to be the result of impending necessity, and of a disposition for conciliation, and that they were agreed to, not for their intrinsic excellence, but as the best system which could be adapted to the circumstances of all, and, at the same time, afford any tolerable prospect of general assent.[8]

These articles were to go into effect when ratified by all the States. Some of the States ratified them promptly; the others held back,[9] and it was not until the 1st day of March, 1781, that they received the assent of all. On the next day Congress assembled under the new government.

This government proved to be "a most unskilful fabric, and totally incompetent to fulfil the ends for which it was erected." It had neither judicial

---

[7] For Articles of Confederation, see Chapter 3 of Book II.
[8] Journal of Congress, Vol. V, p. 208.
[9] For reasons, see "Sketch of the Origin of the Articles of Confederation," Chapter 3 of Book II.

nor executive departments. All its power was
confided to Congress, composed of but one branch.
One of the vital defects was that its laws and
decrees acted on states instead of on individuals;
and it had no power to enforce these laws and
decrees, when violated, except by a resort to arms.
This mode was not practicable.

"Almost as soon as it was ratified," says Kent,
in his Commentaries on American Law, "the States
began to fail in a prompt and faithful obedience
to its laws. As danger receded, instances of neglect became more frequent, and before the peace
of 1783, the inherent imbecility of the government
had displayed itself with alarming rapidity. The
delinquencies of one State became a pretext or
apology for those of another. The idea of supply-
ing the pecuniary exigencies of the nation, from
requisitions on the States, was soon found to be
altogether delusive. The national engagements
seem to have been entirely abandoned. Even the
contributions for the ordinary expenses of the government fell almost entirely upon the two States
which had the most domestic resources. Attempts
were very early made by Congress, and in remon-
strances the most manly and persuasive, to obtain
from the several States the right of levying, for a
limited time, a general impost, for the exclusive
purpose of providing for the discharge of the national debt. It was found impracticable to unite
the States in any provision for the national safety
and honor. Interfering regulations of trade, and
interfering claims of territory, were dissolving the

friendly attachments, and the sense of common interest, which had cemented and sustained the Union during the arduous struggles of the Revolution. Symptoms of distress, and marks of humiliation, were rapidly accumulating. It was with difficulty that the attention of the States could be sufficiently exerted to induce them to keep up a sufficient representation in Congress to form a quorum for business. The finances of the nation were annihilated. The whole army of the United States was reduced, in 1784, to 80 persons; and the States were urged to provide some of the militia to garrison the western posts. In short, to use the language of the authors of The Federalist,[10] 'each State, yielding to the voice of immediate interest or convenience, successively withdrew its support from the Confederation, till the frail and tottering edifice was ready to fall upon our heads, and to crush us beneath its ruins.'"

There was in truth no government worthy the name. Congress could not keep its engagements, and foreign nations would not enter into treaties of commerce with America because of her disunited condition. "We are," said Washington, "one nation to-day, and thirteen to-morrow,—who will treat with us on these terms?"

At the close of the Revolutionary war, Washington retired to his estate at Mount Vernon; and there in his retirement watched with great solici-

---

[10]Alexander Hamilton, James Madison and John Jay were the authors of "The Federalist."

tude the workings of the several parts of the Confederation; anxious to see whether the thirteen States, under the present organization, could form an efficient general government, so as to secure the objects and results of the Revolution. Day by day, however, he was becoming more doubtful of the solidity of the fabric he had assisted in forming.

In a letter to James Warren, of Massachusetts, Washington thus expressed himself as to the Confederation. "The Confederation," he writes, "appears to me to be little more than a shadow without the substance, and Congress a migratory body, their ordinances being little attended to. To me it is a solecism in politics; indeed it is one of the most extraordinary things in nature, that we should confederate as a nation, and yet be afraid to give the rulers of that nation * * * sufficient powers to order and direct the affairs of the same. By such policy as this the wheels of government are clogged, and our brightest prospects, and that high expectation which was entertained of us by the wondering world, are turned into astonishment; and from the high ground on which we stood, we are descending into the vale of confusion and darkness."[11]

Again he expresses himself as to a national policy. "I have ever been a friend," says Washington, "to adequate powers in Congress, without which it is evident to me, we never shall establish a national character, or be considered as on a respect-

[11]Sparks, IX, 139.

able footing by the powers of Europe.— We are
either a united people under one head and for
federal purposes, or we are thirteen independent
sovereignties, eternally counteracting each other.
—If the former, whatever such a majority of the
States as the Constitution points out, conceives to
be for the benefit of the whole, should in my
humble opinion, be submitted to by the minority.—
I can foresee no evil greater than disunion; than
those unreasonable jealousies (I say unreasonable
because I would have a proper jealousy always
awake, and the United States on the watch to
prevent individual States from infracting the Constitution, with impunity) which are continually
poisoning our minds and filling them with imagin-
ary evils for the prevention of real ones."[12]

In a letter to the illustrious patriot, John Jay,[13]
then Secretary of Foreign Affairs, Washington
was of the opinion that public affairs were draw-
ing rapidly to a crisis. "We have errors," said he,
"to correct. We have probably had too good an
opinion of human nature in forming our confederation. Experience has taught us that men will
not adopt and carry into execution measures the
best calculated for their own good, without the
intervention of coercive power. I do not conceive
we can exist long as a nation, without lodging
somewhere, a power which will pervade the whole
Union in as energetic a manner as the authority

[12]Sparks, IX, 121.
[13]The first Chief Justice of the Supreme Court of the United
States, was born in the city of New York, December 12, 1745; died
May 17, 1829.

of the State government extends over the several
States. * * * What a triumph for the advo-   ⸸
cates of despotism to find that we are incapable of
governing ourselves, and that systems, founded on
the basis of equal liberty, are merely ideal and
fallacious! Would to God that wise measures
may be taken in time to avert the consequences
we have but too much reason to apprehend."[14]

Again, in a letter to James Madison he says,
"The consequences of a lax or inefficient government are too obvious to be dwelt upon. Thirteen
sovereignties pulling against each other, and all
tugging at the federal head, will soon bring ruin
on the whole; whereas, a liberal and energetic
Constitution, well checked and well watched, to
prevent encroachments, might restore us to that
degree of respectability and consequence to which
we had the fairest prospect of attaining."[15]

In a letter to Lafayette, in 1783, four years
before the framing of the Constitution by the Convention at Philadelphia, Washington said: "We
are now an independent people, and have yet to
learn political tactics. We are placed among the
nations of the earth, and have a character to establish; but how we shall acquit ourselves time must
discover. The probability is (at least I fear it),
that local or State politics will interfere too much
with the more liberal and extensive plan of government which wisdom and foresight, freed from
the mist of prejudice, would dictate; and that we

14Irving's "Life of Washington," Vol. 3, p. 239.
15Irving's "Life of Washington," Vol. 3, p. 242.

shall be guilty of many blunders in treading this
boundless theatre before we shall have arrived at
any perfection in this art; in a word, that the
experience which is purchased at the price of difficulties and distress, will alone convince us, that
the honor, power, and true interest of this country
must be measured by a continental scale, and that
every departure therefrom weakens the Union,
and may ultimately break the band which holds
us together. To avert these evils, to form a new
Constitution, that will give consistency, stability,
and dignity to the Union, and sufficient power to
the great Council of the Nation for general purposes, is a duty incumbent on every man who
wishes well to his country, and will meet with my
aid as far as it can be rendered in the private
walks of life."

By these and other expressions, Washington,
although in retirement at Mount Vernon, was exercising a powerful influence on national affairs;
after his long service as a soldier, he was now
becoming the statesman, and preparing the way
for a better Constitution and a more effective government. Indeed, he foreshadowed our present
Constitution.

CHAPTER III.

WASHINGTON AND THE CONSTITUTION.

With such a condition of affairs confronting them, Washington, Hamilton,[16] Franklin,[17] Madison, and other patriots of the Revolution, with Washington at their head, sought a remedy; and out of their patriotic efforts the Constitution was framed, and adopted by "We, the people of the United States, in order to form a more perfect union, establish justice, insure domestic tranquility, provide for the common defence, promote the general welfare, and secure the blessings of liberty to ourselves and our posterity."[18] To secure all these, the Articles of Confederation were defective, and hence their enumeration in the preamble to the Constitution.

The Union of the Colonies was made a perpetual Union of States, by the Articles of Confederation; this a "more perfect union," by the Constitution; and finally it was welded into an everlasting union, by loyalty to that Constitution.

[16]Alexander Hamilton, soldier, lawyer, and statesman, was born on the Island of Nevis, British West Indies, in January, 1757. Educated at King's (now Columbia) College, and was distinguished as a good speaker and writer, while yet a lad. Entered the Revolutionary army, and became Washington's favorite aide. He served with great efficiency until the close of the war; and then made the law his profession. He had the most original and constructive mind, probably, of any of the statesmen who framed the Constitution; and to him we are largely indebted for the principles upon which the Constitution was constructed, and for its adoption by the people. Washington made him the first Secretary of the Treasury. Died July 4, 1804, of a wound received in a duel with Aaron Burr.

[17]Benjamin Franklin, an eminent philosopher and statesman, was born in Boston, 1706. He rendered distinguished services to the cause of American independence, and was one of the most eminent of the patriots who framed the Constitution, 1787. He died in Philadelphia, full of years and honors, in 1790.

[18]For Constitution, see Chapter 5 of Book II.

The people, by this Constitution, distributed
their powers among the National and State Governments; and they retained whatever governmental powers remained, after this distribution.
In this division and distribution of powers, the
United States, among other things, guaranteed to
every State in the Union a republican form of
government.[19] And it was agreed that this Constitution and the laws of the United States which
shall be made in pursuance thereof; and all treaties made, or which shall be made under the authority of the United States, shall be the supreme law
of the land; and the judges in every State shall
be bound thereby, anything in the Constitution or
laws of any State to the contrary notwithstanding.[20] By this agreement State Constitutions and
laws, were subordinated to the Constitution of
the United States, its laws, and treaties. They
also provided an arbiter, in cases of conflict,—the
Supreme Court of the United States, whose decisions are final. Thus the people, as between the
State and the Nation, vested supreme sovereignty
in the Government of the United States; hence
paramount allegiance is due the Nation,—it knows
no superior.

In whatever way it may have been brought
about,[21] it is certain that the Constitution was
made by the people of the United States, acting
in their sovereign capacity, for their own guidance

[19]See Section 4, of Article IV, of the Constitution.
[20]Article VI of the Constitution.
[21]See "Sketch of the Origin of the Constitution," Chapter 5 of
Book II.

in exercising their sovereign power, and became
a compact between themselves and every one of
their number. This the people had a right to do;
for since the Revolution, at least, all political sovereignty belongs to the people. The supreme, absolute, and uncontrollable power is in the people
of America. They have the right to make and
unmake constitutions. They exercised this right
in making the Constitution of the United States,
as a substitute for the Articles of Confederation,
the parties to which "were free, sovereign and
independent political communties—each possess-
ing within itself all the powers of legislation and
government, over its own citizens, which any political society can possess."[22] By this instrument the
thirteen orginal States became united together for
certain purposes, and the instrument was styled
"Articles of Confederation and Perpetual Union
between the States." The political body thus
formed was entitled "The United States of America."

This instrument was adopted by the several
States in their corporate capacity. But, in so
doing, they exercised, however, sovereignty which
rightfully belonged to the people. By its provisions an uncontrollable sovereignty was left in
the States. A national government thus organized bore the seeds of its own death. States were
the object of its decrees, instead of individuals, as
under the Constitution; and it had no power to
enforce them.

---

[22]Curtis. "Constitutional History of the United States."

To obviate the many weaknesses of the Confederation, the people reconstructed the fabric of government—both state and national. To one they gave certain powers; to the other certain other powers,—keeping the remainder themselves; the fee simple of all power still belonging to them.

The theory, of John C. Calhoun,[23] of South Carolina, and his followers, that the States, as free, and independent sovereignties, made the Constitution and constituted the National Government their common agent for certain purposes; and that, therefore, a State had the right to withdraw or secede from the Union at pleasure, is not borne out by the facts nor by the law. The framers of the Constitution, understanding the weakness of the Union made by the Articles of Confederation in such manner, avoided that rock of destruction by giving the people of the United States an op-

---

[23]John C. Calhoun was born in South Carolina, 1782. Entered Congress, 1811, and served in both Houses many years. Secretary of War for President Monroe, 1817. Elected Vice-President U. S., 1825; re-elected with President Jackson, 1828, and resigned, 1832, because of the attitude the President assumed against South Carolina when that State attempted to put in force Calhoun's "Nullification" and "Secession" doctrines, on account of a protective tariff law having been passed by Congress which South Carolina thought was detrimental to its interests. Calhoun elected to the Senate of the U. S., 1832. Secretary of State for President Tyler, 1843. Re-elected U. S. Senator, 1845, serving until his death in 1850.

Calhoun taught the doctrine that slavery is "a positive good," an advantage alike to the negro and to his owner; that the States are free and independent sovereignties, and as such made the Constitution; that the States, therefore, had the right to nullify a law of Congress or to secede from the Union. The logical result of his teachings was the Civil War.

Webster, in his great reply to Hayne, in the Senate of the U. S., 1830, and in other speeches, demolished Calhoun's theories, but they still remained the evil genius of the country—and bore the fruit of rebellion. Webster clearly demonstrated that the government of the U. S. is a government proper, established by the people of the U. S., and not a compact between sovereign States; that within its limits it is supreme, and that no branch of government—State or National—except the Supreme Court of the U. S., has the right to determine whether or not it has acted within its limits—from which there is no appeal, but to revolution.

portunity, in their sovereign and aggregate capacity, to adopt a Constitution representing their sovereign power, instead of sovereign States. The Constitution speaks in the name of "We, the people of the United States"; while the Confederation spoke in the name of "free, sovereign and independent States." It is true the people of the United States did not assemble in mass and adopt the Constitution, but they elected representatives from their numbers, in their respective States, who adopted it. This was in harmony with a republican form of government.

This theory of Calhoun's was originated out of a desire to obtain and retain political power for certain purposes, and because of a change in the moral and political philosophy of the South, in the interest of a Power determined to rule the Nation and make it subservient to its own selfish interests. But for this, no such theory would have been originated and advocated with such powerful vehemence and determination, as it was. Its persistent advocacy, and the interests it was intended to promote, bore the fruit of rebellion and civil war.

The People's Government, however, still exists, notwithstanding its internal foes; these grow less and less as the years go by. And the time will come when all shall bow in reverence to it as the best government yet devised by man, because of the great impulse it has given to freedom,—everywhere.

The idea that we are a nation—one people—

undivided and indivisible, should be taught in
every home and school in the Republic. It should
be the central idea of the politics of America.

Soon after the Convention, which framed the
Constitution, had completed its labors, but before
the Constitution had been adopted by the people,
Washington thus expressed himself as to its merits, in a letter written to Lafayette. "It appears
a little short of a miracle," writes he, "that the
delegates from so many States, different from each
other, as you know, in their manners, circumstances, and prejudices, should unite in forming a
system of national government so little liable to
well-founded objections. Nor am I such an enthu-
siastic, partial, or indiscriminating admirer of it,
as not to perceive it is tinctured with some real,
though not radical defects. With regard to the
two great points, the pivots upon which the whole
machine must move, my creed is simply, First, that
the general government is not invested with more
powers than are indispensably necessary to perform the functions of a good government; and
consequently, that no objection ought to be made
against the quantity of power delegated to it.

"Secondly, that these powers, as the appointment of all rulers will forever arise from, and at
short, stated intervals recur to, the free suffrages
of the people, are so distributed among the legislative, executive, and judicial branches into which
the general government is arranged, that it can
never be in danger of degenerating into a monarchy, an oligarchy, an aristocracy, or any other

4

despotic or oppressive form, so long as there shall remain any virtue in the body of the people.

"It will at least be a recommendation to the proposed Constitution, that it is provided with more checks and barriers against the introduction of tyranny, and those of a nature less liable to be surmounted, than any government hitherto instituted among mortals.

"We are not to expect perfection in this world; but mankind in modern times, have apparently made some progress in the science of government. Should that which is now offered to the people of America, be found on experiment less perfect than it can be made, a constitutional door is left open for its amelioration."[24]

Again, after the Constitution had been adopted by the people, Washington said in a letter written to Johnathan Trumbull, "We may with a kind of pious and grateful exultation, trace the finger of Providence through those dark and mysterious events, which first induced the States to appoint a general convention, and then led them, one after another, by such steps as were best calculated to effect the object, into an adoption of the system recommended by the General Convention; thereby, in all human probability, laying a lasting foundation for tranquillity and happiness, when we had but too much reason to fear that confusion and misery were coming rapidly upon us."[25]

In all the trials and vicissitudes through which

[24]Irving's "Life of Washington," Vol. 3, p. 245.
[25]Irving's "Life of Washington," Vol. 3, p. 246-7.

his country had passed, Washington had always
recognized the Supreme Ruler as moving the
hearts of men in favor of liberty, and good government; he attributed deliverance, from evils,
to that Power who guides the destinies of men
and of nations. Indeed, it may be said, that he
traced "the finger of Providence" in all "those
dark and mysterious events," through which the
new Nation had passed. Who will say that he
was not right?

To act well for the state, says Sallust,[26] is glorious; virtue alone confers immortality. That
Washington acted well for the state; that he displayed those virtues which confer immortality has
not been denied to him by his countrymen, nor
by the world. Indeed, the whole world has adopted him as the representative of virtue, of liberty,
and of good government. His name and virtues
will go down through all the ages; though dead
he yet speaks to the Republic, and to mankind.

By the adoption of this new Constitution the
United States of America became a living Nation,
among the nations of the world, with a Republican
form of government; and the formation and adoption of that Constitution will go down in history,
as the crowning act of the fathers of the Republic.

As a tribute to the virtues of Washington, the
people made him the first President under the new
Constitution; thus equipped, the new Republic
started on its great career of progress, on the
fourth day of March, 1789.

[26]A Roman historian, born 86 B. C.

I turn now to consider some matters occurring
during the formation of the Constitution, and others, connected with the welfare of the Republic,
for good or for ill.

CHAPTER IV.

EFFECTS OF THE ORDINANCE OF 1787.

While the Convention which formed the Constitution was in session, in 1787, at Philadelphia,
—where liberty and independence rang out their
first notes to the world,—with Washington as its
President, the Congress of the United States, then
acting under the Articles of Confederation, enacted an Ordinance, which for its far-reaching effects,
on the destiny of the Republic, was only second to
the Constitution itself. That was the Ordinance
of 1787,[27] some of the principles of which had been
enunciated by Thomas Jefferson several years before,—for the organization and government of all
that portion of the national domain northwest of
the Ohio River—a large empire within itself—and
out of which five States were afterwards organized
and admitted to the Union; these were the States
of Ohio, Indiana, Illinois, Michigan, and Wiscon-
sin.

This territory had been ceded to the United
States by Virginia, Connecticut, Massachusetts,
and New York, several years prior to the adoption

[27]For Ordinance 1787, see Chapter 4 of Book II.

of the Constitution of the United States; and the whole region was a vast wilderness and solitude, with some trifling exceptions, upon which no laws, but the laws of nature, had ever operated. Civilization knew it not.

Behold it now with its millions of people, and Chicago—Queen of the Lakes—its great metropolis; where but lately[28] assembled representatives of the nations of the earth, in honor of the Discoverer of the New World, and to witness the marvelous progress of the Republic in civilization.

This wilderness territory gave a grand opportunity to carry out the principles embodied in the Declaration. "No ancient rubbish," says an eminent law writer, "was to be cleared away; no time hallowed prejudices to be overcome. All was open and free, as an unsullied sheet, to receive the best impressions of legislative wisdom. Under such auspices, this Ordinance was drawn up, by the late Nathan Dane, of Massachusetts, almost word for word as it now stands; and for brevity, comprehension, and forecast, it has no superior in the annals of legislation."

"I doubt," says Daniel Webster,[29] "whether one single law of any law-giver, ancient or modern, has produced effects of more distinct, marked, and lasting character than the Ordinance of 1787."

---

[28]1892-93.

[29]Daniel Webster, one of the greatest, if not the greatest of American orators, jurists, and statesmen, was born in Salisbury, New Hampshire, January 18, 1782. At the age of fifteen he entered Dartmouth College, where he graduated. Commenced the study of law in his native village, which he completed in Boston, in 1805. He first practiced his profession near his early home; but, not long after, feeling the necessity of a wider sphere of action, he

By its provisions, this vast territory was dedicated to freedom; while the territory south of the Ohio River was afterwards devoted to slavery; and out of which four States were carved and admitted to the Union. These were the States of Kentucky, Tennessee, Mississippi, and Alabama.[30]

It provided, among other things, that, "There shall be neither slavery nor involuntary servitude in the said Territory otherwise than in the punishment of crimes, whereof the party shall have been duly convicted: Provided, always, That any person escaping into the same, from whom labor or service is lawfully claimed in any one of the original States, such fugitive may be lawfully re-

removed to Portsmouth, where he soon gained a prominent position. In 1812 he was elected to Congress, where he displayed remarkable powers both as a debater and an orator. In 1817 he removed to Boston, and resumed the practice of his profession with the highest distinction. In 1822 he was elected to Congress from Boston; and in 1827 was chosen U. S. Senator, from Massachusetts. From that period he was seldom out of public life, having been twice Secretary of State of the United States in which office he died at Marshfield, October 24, 1852.

Webster's defence of the Union and his exposition of the Constitution, in his great reply to Hayne in the Senate of the U. S., in 1830, has been called "the most remarkable speech ever made in the American Congress." He made Americans realize the inestimable value and sacredness of the Union by this, and other great speeches he made during 1830-1833. He will always be known as the "Great Expounder" of the Constitution.

[30] The Continental Congress, in 1784, proposed a plan for the government of all the Western Territory, then including the whole region west of the original thirteen States, as far south as the thirty-first degree of north latitude. The plan was submitted by a committee, of which Thomas Jefferson was chairman. It contemplated the ultimate division of that territory into seventeen states, eight of them below the latitude of the present city of Louisville, in Kentucky. Among the provisions for the government of that region reported by Jefferson was the following: "That after the year 1800 of the Christian era, there shall be neither slavery nor involuntary servitude in any of the said States, otherwise than in punishment of crimes, whereof the party shall have been convicted to be personally guilty." This clause was stricken out, April 19, 1784, on motion of Mr. Spaight, of North Carolina, seconded by Mr. Read, of South Carolina. A majority of the States were against striking it out, but the Articles of Confederation required a vote of nine States to carry a proposition. July 13, 1787, the Ordinance of 1787 was passed—the final result of the effort made in 1784. See Journals of Congress.

claimed and conveyed to the person claiming his
or her labor or service as aforesaid."[31]

It also provided and declared that, "Religion,
morality and knowledge, being necessary to good
government and the happiness of mankind, schools
and the means of education, shall be forever encouraged."[32]

This was a grand declaration, and fitting to be
laid alongside of the Declaration of Independence,
when we consider that the basis of the best civilization is, religion, morality, and knowledge. The
Northern States encouraged these from the beginning; and the descendants of the Puritans followed in the footsteps of their ancestors, and education was fostered with a jealous care. On the
other hand the Southern States, from the beginning, were adverse to the education of the mass
of their people, who, as an eminent statesman of
our early history says, "are very ignorant and very
poor." During the Colonial days Sir William Ber-
keley, governor of Virginia, an English aristocrat
and a stalwart upholder of the kingly idea of government, said, in alluding to the free schools of
New England, "I thank God there are no free
schools nor printing presses here, and I hope we
shall not have these hundred years. * * * God
keep us from both."

They looked upon education as necessary only
for the aristocracy, and made no provision for
the general education of the people. The children

[31]Article VI.
[32]Article III.

of the wealthy planters, who were possessed of
large numbers of slaves, were either educated in
England or in the institutions of the North; and
this state of affairs was kept up until the Civil
War, with but little, if any, improvement, notwithstanding the warning words of Jefferson,[33] near
a hundred years ago, that free schools were an
essential part—one of the columns, as he expressed
it—of the republican edifice, and that "without
instruction free to all, the sacred flame of liberty
could not be kept burning in the hearts of Americans." But his words, of patriotism and of devo-
tion to freedom, were not heeded.

Slavery seemed more to the South than anything else; and they, in the beginning of our national existence, looked after its interests with a
jealous care,—a care worthy of a better cause.
The compromises made with it, from time to time,
were the result of the tenacity of the South in its
favor. Out of it and these, the South sought to
perpetuate its power in the Nation. The avarice
of the South, on that question, seemed to predom-
inate over its conscience; and as avarice increased,
as it did, conscience decreased; so that the people
of the South, or rather its aristocracy, finally demanded that slavery should become a national institution, and based that demand on the Constitution itself. Well had it been otherwise!

[33]Thomas Jefferson, a great statesman and the third President
of the United States, was born in 1743, at Shadwell, Virginia.
Drafted the Declaration of Independence. Associated with him,
among others, to prepare the Declaration, was John Adams, one
of the great patriots of the Revolution, and second President of
the United States, who was born in Braintree, near Boston, 1735.
Both he and Jefferson died on the 4th of July, 1826.

But I have anticipated somewhat, and turn now, to consider some of the dangers confronting "the fathers" in framing the Constitution, and by that instrument make a more perfect Union.

CHAPTER V.

DANGERS CONFRONTING THE MAKERS OF THE CONSTITUTION AND RESULTS.

The Constitution was the result of mature deliberation on the part of the Convention which framed it, and sent it forth to the people for their ratification. But, strange as it may appear, at the present time, to those who have not given the matter attention, an element of discord was introduced in the formation of the Constitution.

The existence of slavery was one of the chief obstacles,—probably the chief obstacle,—to the formation of the Constitution. It would seem that after making the declaration, "that all men are created equal," and fighting to maintain the same; and the further fact that Congress had declared in the Ordinance of 1787, that, "There shall be neither slavery nor involuntary servitude in the said Territory," such would not have been the case. But so it was.

In the language of Jefferson, "What an incomprehensible machine is man! who can endure toil, famine, strife, imprisonment, and death itself, in vindication of his own liberty, and the next mo-

ment be deaf to all those motives whose power
supported him through his trial, and inflict on his
fellowman a bondage, one hour of which is fraught
with more misery than ages of that which he rose
in rebellion to oppose."

Slavery had been fastened on the colonists,—at
first against their will; but when the time came
to form a national government with a Constitution, which it was hoped would endure forever,
stronger and better adapted to promote the welfare and happiness of the people, than the Articles
of Confederation,—one in harmony with the Declaration,—the delegates did not agree as to what
disposition should be made of slavery, then existing in nearly all the thirteen original States. The
Northern States held but few slaves. Some none;
and those who did have them soon freed them of
their own accord, as they believed slavery to be
wrong, and contrary to the spirit of free institutions.[34] At that time the question of the rightful-
ness of slavery was being agitated to a large extent, not only in this,but in other nations. But,
notwithstanding this, the Southern States looked
with disfavor on the idea of freeing their slaves,

[34]Curtis, in his Constitutional History of the United States, on
page 420, says: "Although, at the time of the formation of the
Constitution, slavery had been expressly abolished in two of the
States only (Massachusetts and New Hampshire), the framers of
that instrument practically treated all but the five Southern States
—Maryland, Virginia, North Carolina, South Carolina, and Georgia
—as if the institution had been already abolished within their
limits, and counted all the colored persons therein, whether bond
or free, as part of the free population; assuming that the eight
Northern and Middle States would be free States, and that the
five Southern States would continue to be slave States. This appears from the whole tenor of the debates, in which the line is
constantly drawn, as between slaveholding and non-slaveholding
States, so as to throw eight States upon the Northern and five
upon the Southern side."

or of wiping out the slave trade, although some of their strongest and best men condemned it; Washington, Madison, and Jefferson among the number.

In 1774, Washington was chairman of a committee which declared in regard to the slave trade: "We take this opportunity to declare our most earnest wish to see an entire stop put to such a wicked, cruel, and unnatural trade."

In 1783, Washington wrote to Lafayette: "The scheme which you propose as a precedent to encourage the emancipation of the black people of this country from the state of bondage in which they are held, is a practical evidence of the benevolence of your heart. I shall be happy to join you in so laudable a work."

Again, in 1786, he wrote Lafayette, "* * * Your late purchase of an estate in the colony of Cayenne, with a view of emancipating the slaves on it, is a generous and noble proof of your humanity. Would to God a like spirit might diffuse itself generally into the minds of the people of this country. But I despair of seeing it. Some petitions were presented to the Assembly (of Virginia), at its last session for the abolition of slavery, but they could scarcely obtain a reading."

And again, in 1786, he wrote Robert Morris: "There is not a man living who wishes more sincerely than I do to see a plan adopted for the abolition of slavery. But there is but one proper and effective mode by which it can be accomplished, and that is by legislative authority, and this, as far as my support will go, shall never be wanting."

In 1787, he wrote Mr. John F. Mercer, of Philadelphia: "1 never mean to possess another slave by purchase. * * * It is among my first wishes to see some plan adopted so that slavery in this country may be abolished by law."

In 1797, Washington wrote his nephew, Lawrence Lewis: "I wish, from my soul, that the Legislature of Virginia could see the policy of the gradual abolition of slavery. It might prevent much future mischief."

Madison[35] said, in regard to the abolition of the slave trade: "The dictates of humanity, the principles of the people, the national safety and happiness, and prudent policy, require it of us. It is to be hoped that by expressing a national disapprobation of the trade, we may destroy it, and save our country from reproaches, and our posterity

[35]James Madison, fourth President of the United States, was born in Virginia, March 16, 1751. Graduate of Princeton College, N. J., 1771. He and Alexander Hamilton of New York, were the foremost of the distinguished statesmen who framed the Constitution. Madison not only drafted the main features of the Constitution, but offered the first ten amendments in Congress. He was strongly in favor of having the Constitution submitted to the people of the United States—as it was—for adoption, instead of the State Legislatures; so that it might make a system of government founded on the consent of the people, and thus be a constitution of government ordained by those who hold the right to exercise all political power; and not a system of government founded by sovereign States, as was the Confederation.

Madison was a member of the first Congress under the Constitution, 1789, continuing as such until 1797. Appointed Secretary of State by President Jefferson, 1801. Elected President of the U. S., 1808. Re-elected for a second term. Died June 28, 1836.

Madison was not a believer in the doctrines of "Secession" and "Nullification"—advocated by Calhoun and his followers. In 1832, he said of the claimed right of a State to withdraw at will from the Union: "It is high time that the claim to secede at will should be put down by the public opinion."

Again, in 1834, he said in regard to nullification: "Nullification has the effect of putting powder under the Constitution, and a match in the hand of every party to blow them up at pleasure." He said nullification and secession "both spring from the same poisonous root."

from the imbecility ever attendant on a country filled with slaves.

`"We have seen the mere distinction of color made, in the most enlightened period of time, a ground of the most oppressive dominion ever exercised by man over man.

"It is wrong to admit into the Constitution the idea that there can be property in man."

Jefferson in his "Notes on Virginia,"[36] 1781, said, "There must, doubtless, be an unhappy influence on the manners of our people produced by the existence of slavery among us. The whole commerce between master and slave is a perpetual exercise of the most boisterous passions, the most unremitting despotism on the one part, and degrading submissions on the other. Our children see this, and learn to imitate it; for man is an imitative animal. This quality is the germ of all education in him. From his cradle to his grave he is learning to do what he sees others do. If a parent could find no motive either in his philanthropy, or his self love, for restraining the intemperance of passion towards his slave, it should always be a sufficient one that his child is present. But generally it is not sufficient. The parent storms, the child looks on, catches the lineaments of wrath, puts on the same airs to the circle of smaller slaves, gives aloose to the worst of passions, and thus nursed, educated, and daily exercised, cannot but be stamped by it with odious peculiarities. The man must be a prodigy who

---

[36]Page 240.

can retain his manners and morals undepraved by such circumstances. And with what execration should the Statesman be loaded, who, permitting one-half the citizens thus to trample on the rights of the other, transforms those into despots, and these into enemies; destroys the morals of the one part, and the amor patriae of the other. For if a slave can have a country in this world, it must be any other in preference to that in which he is born to live and labor for another, in which he must lock up the faculties of his nature, contribute, as far as depends on his individual endeavors, to the evanishment of the human race, or to entail his own miserable condition on the endless generations proceeding from him.

"With the morals of the people their industry also is destroyed. For in a warm climate no man will labor for himself who can make another labor for him. This is so true, that of the proprietors of slaves a very small proportion, indeed, are ever seen to labor.

"And can the liberties of a nation be thought secure when we have removed their only firm basis, a conviction in the minds of the people that these liberties are the gift of God; that they are not to be violated but with his wrath?"

He denounced slavery as "a violation of human rights"; and said that not only honor, but the "best interests of the country" demanded its extinction. "Indeed," said he, "I tremble for my country when I reflect that God is just."

The delegates in that Convention from South

Carolina and Georgia announced, upon the proposal to suppress the slave trade immediately, that if this were done those States would not become part of the Union, for they must have slaves. Rutledge said, "Religion and humanity have nothing to do with this question. Interest alone is the governing principle with nations. The true question at present is whether the Southern States shall or shall not be parties to the Union." Charles C. Pinckney said, "South Carolina can never receive the plan if it prohibit the slave trade." He was an able and strenuous supporter of the interests of the South in all that related to their right to hold and increase their slave population. He contended earnestly against a grant of authority to the general government to prohibit the importation of slaves. Georgia and North Carolina took the same position.

This was not the first time that South Carolina and Georgia had taken a stand in favor of the slave trade, and determined that they would not agree to anything which looked towards a discontinuance of it. When the Declaration of Independence was under consideration in the Continental Congress, the following clause in the original draft of the Declaration, reprobating the enslaving the inhabitants of Africa, was struck out in complaisance to South Carolina and Georgia, who had never attempted to restrain the importation of slaves, and who, on the contrary, still wished to continue it:[37]

[37]Jefferson's Writings, Vol. I, p. 15.

"He (George III[38]) has waged cruel war against human nature itself, violating its most sacred rights of life and liberty in the persons of a distant people who never offended him, captivating and carrying them into slavery in another hemisphere, or to incur miserable death in their transportation thither. This piratical warfare, the opprobrium of infidel powers, is the warfare of the Christian king of Great Britain. Determined to keep open a market where men should be bought and sold, he has prostituted his negative for suppressing every legislative attempt to prohibit or restrain this execrable commerce. And that this assemblage of horrors might want no fact of distinguished dye, he is now exciting those very people to rise in arms among us, and to purchase that liberty of which he has deprived them, by murdering the people on whom he has obtruded them; thus paying off former crimes committed against the liberties of one people, with crimes which he urges them to commit against the lives of another."

That was a critical time, and because of the opposition of those States, that clause was stricken out of the Declaration. But a still more critical time was now at hand. If the new Nation, which had so recently achieved its independence, after so long a struggle, did not form a Constitution stronger and better than the Articles of Confederation,—a more perfect Union,—in all probability the Republic would cease to exist, and each State

[38]King of England.

would form a Nation of its own. This could not be,—must not be! The Union must be formed or else all their labor for freedom and independence be in vain. So out of the necessities of the case a compromise was made with slavery,—broader, and one with far more reaching effects, than the first concession made by the Ordinance of 1787. This compromise was made a part of the Constitution, but the word "slave" or "slavery" was not used in making it. The concessions made were three, as follows:

First.—Representatives and direct taxes shall be apportioned among the several States which may be included within this Union, according to their respective numbers, which shall be determined by adding to the whole number of free persons, including those bound to service for a term of years, and excluding Indians not taxed, three-fifths of all other persons.[39]

Second.—The migration or importation of such persons as any of the States now existing shall think proper to admit shall not be prohibited by the Congress prior to the year one thousand eight hundred and eight; but a tax or duty may be imposed on such importation, not exceeding ten dollars for each person.[40]

Third.—No person held to service or labor in one State, under the laws thereof, escaping into another, shall, in consequence of any law or regulation therein, be discharged from such service or labor, but shall be delivered up on claim of the

[39]See Section 2, Article I, of Constitution.
[40]See Section 9, Article I, of Constitution.

party to whom such service or labor may be due.[41]

By these forced concessions the obstacles to the formation of the Union were removed. The result of that compromise was the recognition of slavery by the Constitution.

Thus the Republic was built upon two antagonistic civilizations, the germs of which had long before been planted. From that time on these two civilizations developed rapidly; and in that development they grew more and more antagonistic, as might be expected, for one was founded on "right"; and the other on "wrong."

The time came when the one or the other of these civilizations must prevail. Both could not exist under the same flag, and in the same country. They met amid the clash of arms, and the "right" triumphed. In that conflict our country became a great battlefield, and the spirit of freedom and union was triumphant over the spirit of slavery and disunion.

A civilization based on a "wrong" cannot endure. Justice is sure and is meted out to states' and nations as well as to individuals. The rendering of the decree may be long delayed. But it is one of the immutable laws of the "higher power,"—to which all are subject,—that sooner or later the decree will be entered. So it was in the history of our Republic. In its evolution the forces of right and wrong long contended; but finally the decree went forth enforcing the declaration and the law, that all men are created equal.

[41]See Section 2, Article IV, of Constitution.

PART II.

CHAPTER I.

PLANTING GERMS AND SOME RESULTS.

The faith of one man,—Columbus,—and the faith of one woman,—Queen Isabella,—in that man, gave opportunity for the founding of a Republic in the New World, on a large scale, based upon the principle that all men are created equal.

Every age has produced great men. But it was left for the eighteenth and nineteenth centuries to bring forth men imbued with the spirit of liberty to all mankind. The eighteenth century produced a Washington; the nineteenth a Lincoln. Both firmly believed in a government "of the people, by the people, and for the people"; that all men are created equal, and that freedom,—both civil and religious,—is the natural right of man.

Washington became the founder of such a government,—our Republic,—and Lincoln its preserver.

The history of a great Republic, like ours, should be the study of all who love liberty. This Republic has no parallel in the history of nations. Indeed, it stands out unique and alone as the only

Republic which fully illustrates constitutional liberty in all its beneficence, power, and grandeur.

There ever has been, and probably ever will be, a conflict going on between "right" and "wrong." But, sometime the right triumphs over the wrong. The day of triumph may be long delayed, but come it will. ·

This Republic was not born and reared without a conflict. It has grown to its present greatness through the blood of its people. They were willing to offer themselves as a sacrifice that all might enjoy freedom,—both civil and religious. The sacrifice has been made; and behold, a land where all enjoy that freedom!

Let us inquire as to the evolutionary process of the formation of our present Republic. Its formation began during the early part of the seventeenth century. During that century the germs of two diverse and antagonistic civilizations were planted in this country. One on the rocky shores of Massachusetts, by a race descended from the Saxon; the other in Virginia, by an English aristocracy, the descendants of the Norman Cavalier. The first was founded on the principle of freedom to all; the second, on the idea that some are born to rule, others to serve.

It needs no argument, at this late day, to prove that that civilization based on freedom was right; and that the other based on slavery was wrong.

For over two centuries these two civilizations developed side by side. In that development each

produced fruit according to its kind. The one good
fruit and the other bad.

As the course of Empire turned westward,
these two civilizations moved out side by side
towards the setting sun. The descendants of the
Puritan hewed a way through the wilderness for
the march of liberty, equality, and human rights;
the followers of the Cavalier led a mournful pro-
cession to the music of the sad song of the slave.

Human avarice brought the slave and the
slaveholder to the shores of the New World, and
this was the result.

Our history may be divided into four periods.
The first, the Colonial, while we were under the
control of England; the second, the Revolutionary, wherein we gained our independence by arms;
the third, the Union of the States into a government; and the fourth, the maintenance of that
Union by arms.

The history of these four periods shows the
foundation upon which our Republic rests, its
strength, and probable perpetuity.

During the Colonial period there was a bond
of sympathy between the people of these diverse
civilizations, in that both were desirous of throw-
ing off the yoke of the common oppressor,—England,—and they united to free themselves from
that oppressor.

On the fourth day of July, 1776, their representatives promulgated the Great Charter of our
Independence, announcing to the world, "that all
men are created equal; that they are endowed by

their Creator with certain inalienable rights; that among these are life, liberty, and the pursuit of happiness." They concluded that great instrument by declaring, "that these United Colonies are, and of right ought to be, free and independent States; that they are absolved from all allegiance to the British Crown, and that all political connection between them and the state of Great Britain is, and ought to be, totally dissolved."[1] And, for the support of this declaration, with a firm reliance on the protection of Divine Providence, they mutually pledged to each other their lives, their fortunes, and their sacred honor.

Washington and his compatriots fought to maintain that declaration, and, after an heroic struggle, won. Thus by the Declaration and the arbitrament of war, the United Colonies became "free and independent States." Free and independent of Great Britain, but not, however, free and independent of each other. For at the beginning of that struggle they united, first, as Colonies; second, as States into a Confederacy;[2] and finally, after the struggle was over, entered into a "more perfect union" by the Constitution of the United States, adopted by the people of all the States.[3] Thus the United States became a nation, among the nations of the world, with a republican form of government.

At the time of the formation of the Union and the adoption of the Constitution, in 1787-8, slavery

---

[1]For Declaration of Independence, see Chapter 2 of Book II.
[2]For Articles of Confederation, see Chapter 3 of Book II.
[3]For Constitution, see Chapter 5 of Book II.

existed in nearly all of the States to a greater or
less extent. There were but few slaves in any of
the Northern States—the great bulk of them being
in the Southern States. The Northern States soon
did away with slavery, but the South still continued it; although it is a well known historical
fact that the fathers of the Republic regarded
slavery as an evil and hoped it would be abolished
by all the States. At the time of the adoption of
the Constitution, they saw no other way, under
the circumstances, than to trust its extirpation to
the people, believing that, in time, they would vol-
untarily do away with it. But, in this, they were
mistaken.

Alexander H. Stephens, of Georgia, said in
1861: "The prevailing ideas entertained by him
(Jefferson) and most of the leading statesmen at
the time of the formation of the Constitution were,
that the enslavement of the African was in violation of the laws of nature; that it was wrong in
principle, socially, morally and politically. It
was an evil they knew not well how to deal with;
but the general opinion of the men of that day
was, that, somehow or other, in the order of providence, the institution would be evanescent and
pass away. This idea, though not incorporated in
the Constitution, was the prevailing idea at the
time. The Constitution, it is true, secured every
guarantee to the institution while it should last,
and hence no argument can be justly used against
the Constitutional guarantees thus secured, because of the common sentiment of the day. Those

ideas, however, were fundamentally wrong. They
rested upon the assumption of the equality of the
races. This was an error." * * * "The negro
by nature, or by the curse against Canaan, is fitted
for that condition which he occupies in our system." "The negro," said Mr. Stephens, "is not
equal to the white man"; and, "slavery, subordination to the superior race, is his natural and normal condition. It is, indeed, in conformity with
the ordinance of the Creator. It is not for us to
inquire into the wisdom of His ordinances or to
question them."

Although all the Northern States did away
with slavery, and Washington and others of the
founders of the Republic, living in Southern
States, freed their slaves, yet the people of the
Southern States, or rather its aristocracy, retained it and nursed it with a jealous care, and
began to advocate the idea that they could not
get along without it, and that the ideas of the
"fathers" were "fundamentally wrong." This idea,
and their jealousy of the institution, grew in in-
tensity as the years rolled by. Thus, a slaveholding aristocracy grew up in the Republic very dangerous to its existence. For this aristocracy subordinated everything to its own selfish interests.

In 1838 a distinguished Representative from
South Carolina, declared, in the Congress of the
United States, that "many worthy men, who were
formerly somewhat uneasy at the existence of
this institution, now feel themselves called upon
by every motive, personal and private, by every

consideration, public and patriotic, to guard it with the most jealous watchfulness,—to defend it at every hazard." These were the sentiments of all those in the South who had embraced the new moral and political philosophy of John C. Calhoun, Robt. Y. Hayne,[4]—with whom Webster had his great debate in 1830,—and others, who were seeking to perpetuate slavery and its power in the Nation.

This slaveholding aristocracy became arrogant and tyrannical,—as all aristocracies do. It controlled the State governments of the South, and largely dominated in the councils of the Nation, aided by a portion of the people of the North who were in sympathy with them and belonged to the same political party. Although the State governments of the South were republican in name, in fact they were oligarchies.

In consequence of this state of things the common people of the South were in degradation,—even lower than the slaves,—and exercised no influence in governmental affairs; these being entirely in the hands of the slaveholding aristocracy. Labor was degraded, and the free laborer was regarded as being lower than the slave. For a white man to labor was considered a degradation. Public education was neglected, and, indeed,

---

[4]Robert Y. Hayne was born near Charleston, S. C., in 1791. Became a lawyer and orator. United States Senator for ten years. In the debate with Webster in the United States Senate, in 1830, advocated the doctrine that the States are sovereign, and have the right to nullify an act of Congress. Chairman of Committee of the South Carolina Convention which reported the nullification ordinance, 1832. Soon after was elected Governor of South Carolina. Issued a counter manifesto to President Jackson's proclamation. Died 1841.

hardly known; consequently the great mass of the
people grew up in ignorance. Not so in the North.
There education was fostered, its people were educated, labor was encouraged, and the dignity of
labor recognized. Education and labor went hand
in hand. In consequence the laborer had a chance
to rise. He took part in matters of government,
and his voice was heard in the Councils of the
State and Nation.

These differences between the two sections
grew out of the difference of their civilizations—
the one being based on freedom; the other on
slavery.

In the formation of the Union, the slave power
got the advantage. Slavery was indirectly recognized in the Constitution; and in fixing the basis
of representation each State should have in Congress, five slaves were counted as three freemen,
although they were held as property.[5]

With this advantage, and with the idea that
they were the ruling class, this slaveholding aristocracy grew arrogant and tyrannical and sought
to control the Government and subordinate it entirely to their own interests.

It seems to be one of the attributes of wrong
that it is aggressive and on the alert. It is impatient of restraint and restriction, and is ever seeking to enlarge its borders.

The slaveholders were alert, aggressive, and
impatient of restraint or restriction. They sought
to perpetuate slavery by extending it into the Ter-

---

[5]See Section 2 of Article I, the Constitution.

ritories of the United States. They were not satis-
fied with having it confined to the States where
it already existed. Their selfishness, and the moral
degradation which the institution of slavery had
fastened on them, led them—to give a sort of color
to their claimed right of perpetuating and extending it—to advocate it as a "divine institution." In
other words, that the same Creator who made man
in his own image, declared that it is right for one
man to enslave another. Even ministers of the
Gospel proclaimed that doctrine; and bought and
sold their fellow men.

Bishop Meade wrote a book of sermons to be
used for slaves. In one he says, "Almighty God
hath been pleased to make you slaves here, and
to give you nothing but labor and poverty in this
world. * * * This rule you should always
carry in your mind, that is, that you should do all
service for your masters as if you did it for God
himself. * * * Your masters and mistresses
are God's overseers. * * * You are to do all
service to them as unto Christ. Failing to do this,
you will be turned over to the devil to become his
slave forever in hell." And this in the nineteenth
century of the Christian era!

They pretended not to believe the declaration
that all men are created equal. Working themselves by degrees into that belief, they sought to
extend the "institution" by fastening it on the
Territories of the United States; thus making it a
national instead of a local institution.

In this they succeeded for many years, by their

aggressiveness and persistency. During that time compromise after compromise was made with slavery, and always to the advantage of the slaveholders. Thus they acquired a power almost resistless. At last, however, the conscience of the Nation became so aroused that the lovers of freedom determined, if possible, to stem the onflowing tide and stop its further spread.

When, therefore, in 1854, Kansas and Nebraska were organized into Territories by Congress, the conflict came on with renewed vigor; and the question of the right of extending slavery was agitated with vehemence. Freedom was aroused against slavery as never before. The question arose, Shall the public domain of the Republic be the theater of all free or all slave labor? It was evident that one or the other of these must prevail, for the antagonism was so great between them that one or the other must yield. The slave power sounded the trumpet for battle, and the newly organized Territory of Kansas was its chosen field of conflict.

The champions of freedom claimed that this Nation was not founded with the idea of perpetuating and extending slavery; that it was a great wrong; that freedom was the normal condition of man; and that the public domain of this country was set apart for freedom. It was not proposed to interfere with slavery as it existed,—but it must not be extended; and no more compromises must be made, that too many had already been made with it.

CHAPTER II.

THE LINCOLN-DOUGLAS DEBATE.

While this great struggle, between freedom and slavery, was going on in Kansas, Stephen A. Douglas[6] and Abraham Lincoln, opposing candidates for the United States Senate in Illinois, held, in 1858, a series of debates, and discussed the issue then uppermost in the minds of the people.

Mr. Douglas was the champion of the slavery side of the question, and Mr. Lincoln the champion of the side of freedom. Both were able representative men, although Mr. Lincoln was but little known to the country. These debates developed the claims of both parties, and attracted the attention of the Nation. I can do no better than to here give the leading points of their claims.

Mr. Douglas said: "I hold that the signers of the Declaration of Independence had no reference to negroes at all when they declared all men to be created equal. * * * They alluded to men of European birth and European descent,—to white men, and to none others, when they declared

"Stephen A. Douglas was born in Vermont, 1813; removed to Illinois in 1831. Taught school, studied law, was Attorney General of the State, Secretary of State, Judge of the Supreme Court, Congressman, United States Senator, and finally ran for President against Abraham Lincoln, as one of the Democratic candidates; John C. Breckenridge, of Kentucky, being the other. Died June 3, 1861. After Mr. Lincoln was inaugurated as President, he heartily supported the Union cause, and when dying he breathed a prayer that the enemies of his country might be overthrown. With this record, contrast that of John C. Breckenridge. Born in Kentucky, 1821. Studied law; served in the Mexican war; elected to Congress, 1851; re-elected, 1853. Elected Vice-President of the United States on ticket with James Buchanan, 1856. Elected U. S. Senator, 1860. Defended the Southern Confederacy in the Senate. Expelled from the Senate, December, 1861. Appointed Major-General in the Confederate army and served in the field until February, 1865, when Jefferson Davis appointed him Secretary of War. Died, 1875.

that doctrine. I hold that this Government was established on the white basis. It was established by white men for the benefit of white men and their posterity forever, and should be administered by white men, and none others. But it does not follow, by any means, that merely because he is not our equal, that, therefore, he should be a slave. * * *

"If the people of Kansas want a slave State, they have a right, under the Constitution of the United States, to form such a State, and I will let them come into the Union with slavery or without, as they determine. If the people of any other Territory desire slavery, let them have it. If they do not want it, let them prohibit it. It is their business, not mine. It is none of our business in Illinois whether Kansas is a free State or a slave State. * * * I assert that this Government can exist as they (the fathers) made it, divided into free and slave States, if any one State chooses to retain slavery.

"He (Lincoln) says that he looks forward to a time when slavery shall be abolished everywhere. * * * I look forward to a time when each State shall be allowed to do as it pleases. If it chooses to keep slavery forever, it is none of my business, but its own; if it chooses to abolish slavery, it is its own business—not mine. I care more for the great principle of self government, the right of the people to rule, than I do for all the negroes in Christendom. I would not endanger the perpetuity of the Union, I would not blot

out the great inalienable rights of the white men
for all the negroes that ever existed. Hence, I
say, let us maintain this Government on the principles that our fathers made it, recognizing the
right of each State to keep slavery as long as its
people determine, or to abolish it when they
please. * * *

"His (Lincoln's) idea is that he will prohibit
slavery in all the Territories and thus force them
all to become free States, surrounding the slave
States with a cordon of free States and hemming
them in, keeping the slaves confined to their present limits whilst they go on multiplying until the
soil on which they live will no longer feed them,
and he will thus be able to put slavery in a course
of ultimate extinction by starvation. * * *
He intends to do that in the name of humanity
and Christianity, in order that we may get rid of
the terrible crime and sin entailed upon our fathers of holding slaves. * * * I ask you to look
into these things, and then tell me whether the
Democracy or the Abolitionists are right. I hold
that the people of a Territory, like those of a
State (I use the language of Mr. Buchanan in his
letter of acceptance) have the right to decide for
themselves whether slavery shall or shall not exist within their limits. * * * My friends, if,
as I have said before, we will only live up to this
great fundamental principle, there will be peace
between the North and South."

Mr. Lincoln said: "You have heard him (Doug-

las) frequently allude to my controversy with him
in regard to the Declaration of Independence. * *

"It may be,argued that there are certain conditions that make necessities and impose them
upon us, and to the extent that a necessity is imposed upon a man he must submit to it. I think
that was the condition in which we found ourselves
when we established this Government. We had
slaves among us, we could not get our Constitution unless we permitted them to remain in slavery, we could not secure the good we did secure
if we grasped for more; and having by necessity
submitted to that much it does not destroy the
principle that that is the charter of our liberties.
Let the charter remain as our standard. * * *

"I think the authors of that notable instrument intended to include all men, but they did not
mean to declare all men equal in all respects.
They did not mean to say all men were equal in
color, size, intellect, moral development or social
capacity. They defined with tolerable distinctness
in what they did consider all men created equal—
equal in certain inalienable rights, among which
are life, liberty, and the pursuit of happiness. This
they said, and this they meant. They did not
mean to assert the obvious untruth, that all
were then actually enjoying that equality, or yet,
that they were about to confer it immediately upon
them. In fact, they had no power to confer such
a boon. They meant simply to declare the right
so that the enforcement of it might follow as fast
as circumstances should permit. They meant to

set up a standard maxim for free society which should be familiar to all; constantly looked to, constantly labored for, and even, though never perfectly attained, constantly approximated, and thereby constantly spreading and deepening its influence and augmenting the happiness and value of life to all people, of all colors, everywhere. * *

"I assert that Judge Douglas and all his friends may search the whole records of the country, and it will be a matter of great astonishment to me if they shall be able to find that one human being three years ago had ever uttered the astounding sentiment that the term "all men" in the Declaration did not include the negro. Do not let me be misunderstood. I know that more than three years ago there were men who, finding this assertion constantly in the way of their schemes to bring about the ascendency and perpetuation of slavery, denied the truth of it. I know that Mr. Calhoun and all the politicians of his school denied the truth of the Declaration. I know that it ran along in the mouth of some Southern men for a period of years, ending at last in that shameful though rather forcible declaration of Pettit of Indiana, upon the floor of the United States Senate, that the Declaration of Independence was in that respect 'a self evident lie,' rather than a self evident truth. But I say, with a perfect knowledge of all this hawking at the Declaration without directly attacking it, that three years ago there never had lived a man who had ventured to assail it in the sneaking way of pretending to believe it

6

and then asserting it did not include the negro. I believe the first man who ever said it was Chief Justice Taney in the Dred Scott case, and the next to him was our friend Stephen A. Douglas. And now it has become the catchword of the entire party. I would like to call upon his friends everywhere to consider how they have come in so short a time to view this matter in a way so entirely different from their former belief? to ask whether they are not being borne along by an irresistible current—whither, they know not? * * *

"Hear what Mr. Clay[7] said: 'It is a general declaration in the act announcing to the World the independence of the thirteen American Colonies, that all men are created equal. Now as an abstract principle, there is no doubt of the truth of that declaration; and it is desirable, in the original construction of society; and in organized societies, to keep it in view as a great fundamental principle. * * * I desire no concealment of my opinions in regard to the institution of slavery. I look upon it as a great evil, and deeply lament that we have derived it from the parental Government, and from our ancestors. But here they are, and the question is, how can they be best dealt with? If a state of nature existed, and we were about to lay the foundations of society, no man would be more strongly opposed than I should be,

---

[7]Henry Clay, lawyer, orator and statesman, was born in Virginia in 1777; died at Washington, D. C., 1852. In 1797 he removed to Lexington, Kentucky. In 1799, when the people of Kentucky were about adopting a State constitution, Clay urged them (but without success) to abolish slavery. He entered Congress in 1806, and continued in public life from that time until his death.

to incorporating the institution of slavery among its elements.'

"What have I done, that I have not the license of Henry Clay's illustrious example here in doing? Have I done aught that I have not his authority for, while maintaining that in organizing new Territories and societies, this fundamental principle should be regarded, and in organized society holding it up to the public view and recognizing what he recognized as the great principle of free government? And when this new principle—this new proposition that no human being ever thought of three years ago—is brought forward, I combat it as having an evil tendency, if not an evil design. I combat it as having a tendency to dehumanize the negro—to take away from him the right of ever striving to be a man. I combat it as being one of the thousand things constantly done in these days to prepare the public mind to make property, and nothing but property, of the negro in all the States of this Union.   *   *   *

"The principle upon which I have insisted in this canvass, is in relation to laying the foundations of new societies. It is nothing but a miserable perversion of what I have said, to assume that I have declared Missouri, or any other slave State, shall emancipate her slaves. I have proposed no such thing. But when Mr. Clay says that in laying the foundations of societies in our Territories where it does not exist, he would be opposed to the introduction of slavery as an element, I insist that we have his warrant—his license for insisting

upon the exclusion of that element which he declared in such strong and emphatic language was
most hateful to him. * * *

"We are now far into the fifth year since a
policy was initiated with the avowed object and
confident promise of putting an end to the slavery
agitation. Under the operation of this policy, that
agitation has not only not ceased, but has constantly augmented. In my opinion, it will not
cease until a crisis shall have been reached and
passed. 'A house divided against itself cannot
stand.' I believe this Government cannot endure
permanently half slave and half free. I do not
expect the house to fall—but I do expect it will
cease to be divided. It will become all one thing
or all the other. Either the opponents of slavery
will arrest the further spread of it, and place it
where the public mind shall rest in the belief that
it is in the course of ultimate extinction, or its
advocates will push it forward till it shall become
alike lawful in all the States—old as well as new,
North as well as South. * * *

"I entertain the opinion upon evidence sufficient to my mind, that the fathers of this Government placed that institution where the public mind
did rest in the belief that it was in the course of
ultimate extinction. Let me ask why they made
provision that the source of slavery—the African
slave trade—should be cut off at the end of twenty
years?[8] Why did they make provision that in all
the new territory we owned at that time, slavery

[8]See Constitution, Section 9 of Article I.

should be forever inhibited?⁰ Why stop its spread
in one direction and cut off its source in another,
if they did not look to its being placed in the course
of ultimate extinction? * * *

"Language is used (in the Constitution) not
suggesting that slavery existed or that the black
race were among us. And I understand the contemporaneous history of those times to be that
covert language was used with a purpose, and that
purpose was that our Constitution, which it was
hoped and is still hoped will endure forever—when
it should be read by intelligent and patriotic men,
after the institution of slavery had passed from
among us—there should be nothing on the face of
the great charter of liberty suggesting that such
a thing as negro slavery had ever existed among
us. This is part of the evidence that the fathers of
the Government expected and intended the institution of slavery to come to an end. They expected and intended that it should be in the course
of ultimate extinction. * * *

"We might, by arresting the further spread of
it, and placing it where the fathers originally
placed it, rest in the belief that it was in the
course of ultimate extinction. Thus the agitation
may cease. * * *

"It is not true that our fathers, as Judge Douglas assumes, made this Government part slave and
part free. Understand the sense in which he puts
it. He assumes that slavery is a rightful thing

⁰North-Western Territory. See Ordinance of 1787, for prohibi-
tion of slavery in that Territory.

within itself—was introduced by the framers of
the Constitution. The exact truth is, that they
found the institution existing among us, and they
left it as they found it. But in making the Government they left this institution with many clear
marks of disapprobation upon it. They found
slavery among them, and they left it among them
because of the difficulty—the absolute impossibil-
ity of its immediate removal. And when Judge
Douglas asks me cannot we let it remain part
slave and part free, as the fathers made it, he
asks a question based upon an assumption which
is of itself a falsehood; and I turn upon him and
ask him the question, when the policy that the
fathers of the Government had adopted in relation
to this element among us was the best policy in
the world—the only wise policy—the only policy
that we can ever safely continue upon—that will
ever give us peace, unless this dangerous element
masters us all and becomes a national institution
—I turn upon him and ask him why he could not
leave it alone. I turn and ask him why he was
driven to the necessity of introducing a new policy
in regard to it. He has himself said he introduced
a new policy.[10] * * * I have proposed nothing more than a return to the policy of the
fathers. * * *

"The Judge alludes very often in the course of
his remarks to the exclusive right which the States
have to decide the whole thing for themselves. I
agree with him very readily that the different

[10]Kansas-Nebraska Bill, in 1854.

States have that right. He is but fighting a man
of straw when he assumes that I am contending
against the right of the States to do as they please
about it. Our controversy with him is in regard to
the new Territories. We have no power as citizens of the free States or in our federal capacity
as members of the Federal Union through the
General Government, to disturb slavery in the
States where it exists. * * *

"The real issue in this controversy—the one
pressing upon every mind—is the sentiment on the
part of one class that looks upon the institution
of slavery as a wrong and of another class that
does not look upon it as a wrong. * * *

"On this subject of treating it as a wrong and
limiting its spread, let me say a word. Has anything ever threatened the existence of this Union
save and except this very institution of slavery?
What is it that we hold most dear among us?
Our own liberty and prosperity. What has ever
threatened our liberty and prosperity, save and
except this institution of slavery? If this is true,
how do you propose to improve the condition of
things by enlarging slavery—by spreading it out
and making it bigger? * * * That is no proper way of treating what you regard a wrong. You
see this peaceful way of dealing with it as a wrong
—restricting the spread of it, and not allowing it
to go into new countries where it has not already
existed. That is the peaceful way, the old fash-
ioned way, the way in which the fathers themselves set us the example. * * *

"Judge Douglas contends that whatever community wants slaves has a right to have them. So they have if it is not a wrong. But if it is a wrong, he cannot say people have a right to do wrong. He says that upon the score of equality, slaves should be allowed to go in a new Territory, like other property. This is strictly logical if there is no difference between it and other property. If it and other property are equal, his argument is entirely logical. But if you insist that one is wrong and the other right, there is no use to institute a comparison between right and wrong. * *

"That is the real issue. That is the issue that will continue in this country when these poor tongues of Judge Douglas and myself shall be silent. It is the eternal struggle between these two principles—right and wrong—throughout the world. They are the two principles that have stood face to face from the beginning of time; and will ever continue to struggle. The one is the common right of humanity and the other the divine right of kings. It is the same principle in whatever shape it develops itself. It is the same spirit that says, 'You work and toil and earn bread, and I'll eat it.' No matter in what shape it comes, whether from the mouth of a king who seeks to bestride the people of his own nation and live by the fruit of their labor, or from one race of men as an apology for enslaving another race, it is the same tyrannical principle."

CHAPTER III.

THE NEW CHAMPION OF FREEDOM.

Those words, of Abraham Lincoln, will go ringing down the ages as long as liberty and free government have an existence. His argument was
made in the light of a broad humanity; in the
light of the true sense of the Declaration of Independence; in the light of the Constitution and
the history of the formation of our Government.
His logic was unanswerable. He spoke with the
vision of a prophet,—as one having authority.

We may well inquire, Who was this new and
powerful champion of freedom? Was he of the
blood royal? Was he born in a palace? Neither.
Born in a cabin of poor and humble parents,[11]
raised amid the surroundings of hardship and poverty incident to a new country; self educated.
Product of the unexhausted West. "Nothing of
Europe here. New birth of our new soil." A
stalwart man imbued with the spirit of liberty to
all mankind; and,—

> "Limbed like the old heroic breeds,
> Who stands self-poised on manhood's solid earth,
> Not forced to frame excuses for his birth,
> Fed from within with all the strength he needs."[12]

This new man Providence raised up for a great

---

[11]Abraham Lincoln was born in Hardin County, Kentucky, February 12, 1809. In 1816 the Lincoln family moved to Spencer County,
Indiana; and, in 1830, to Illinois. In 1834 Abraham Lincoln began
the study of law, and in 1837, began its practice in Springfield, Ill.,
where he remained until he became President of the United States
in 1861. He was re-elected President in 1864. Assassinated by John
Wilkes Booth, April 14, 1865, at Washington, D. C., and died the
following day.
[12]From Lowell's "Commemoration Ode."

purpose. That purpose was to lead the Nation through an irrepressible conflict,—a conflict between two antagonistic civilizations,—that the demands of the Higher Law, upon which the Declaration was based, might be fulfilled. Under him freedom, everywhere, was to receive a new impetus—a new baptism, and finally to be triumphant. He was taking up the great work begun and carried forward by a Garrison, a Phillips and others, who, for many years, had been battling for the rights of man in educating the conscience of the Nation. These re-enforced by Charles Sumner,[13] William H. Seward and others in Congress. He was destined, under Providence, to finish the work they had so well begun and carried forward. This is the man who was to lead the Republic through the fiery furnace of war, and at last to receive the veneration of a grateful people, and the homage of kings and emperors.

The aristocracy of the South had no love for such a man. He was not of their kind. His blows against slavery were felt; and no man had made

---

[13]Charles Sumner was born in Boston, Mass., January 6, 1811. Graduated at Harvard College and Cambridge Law School. Admitted to the bar, 1834. Delivered his first great oration, on the "True Grandeur of Nations," at Boston July 4, 1845; and his first anti-slavery speech, 1850. On the death of Judge Story of the Supreme Court of the United States, in 1845, was offered the vacant seat, but declined. In the winter of 1851 was elected to the Senate of the United States from Massachusetts, to fill the vacancy caused by the resignation of Daniel Webster; retained that position until his death, March 11, 1874.

Of Sumner, Senator George F. Hoar, himself a statesman of large ability, wrote in 1894: "If we judge him by the soundness of his principles, by the wisdom of his measures, by his power to command the support of the people, by the great public results he accomplished, there is no statesman of his time to be named in the same breath with him, save Abraham Lincoln. * * * His figure will abide in History like that of St. Michael in Art, an emblem of celestial purity, of celestial zeal, of celestial courage. It will go down to immortality with its foot upon the dragon of Slavery, and with the sword of the spirit in its hand, but with a tender light in its eye, and a human love in its smile."

so profound an impression on the conscience of
the Nation, as to the wrong of slavery and its
relation to the Government, as he. He stripped
the slaveholders' pretenses naked; and alarmed
them when he said, " 'A house divided against
itself cannot stand.' I believe this Government
cannot endure permanently half slave and half
free. I do not expect the house to fall—but I do
expect it will cease to be divided. It will become
all one thing or all the other. Either the opponents of slavery will arrest the further spread of
it, and place it where the public mind shall rest
in the belief that it is in the course of ultimate
extinction, or its advocates will push it forward
till it shall become alike lawful in all the States—
old as well as new, North as well as South."

It was evident that the course of events was
tending towards one or the other of these alter-
natives, and had been for several years. It was
almost certain to "become all one thing or all the
other." The slave power had been encouraged to
believe that slavery would become a national institution by the Fugitive Slave Law of 1850, the
Kansas-Nebraska Act of 1854, and later, 1857, by
the decision of the Supreme Court of the United
States in the Dred Scott case, wherein Chief Justice Taney[14] announced that the Missouri Compro-

---

[14]Roger Brooke Taney was born in Maryland, March 17, 1777.
Admitted to the bar as a lawyer in 1799. He served in the Senate
and Assembly of Maryland. Appointed Attorney General of the
United States in 1831, and Secretary of the Treasury in 1833. He
was appointed Chief Justice of the United States on the death of
Judge Marshall, and took his seat as such in January, 1837, and
remained in that office until his death, in the city of Washington,
on October 12, 1864, when his place was filled by Salmon P. Chase,
of Ohio, who was appointed by President Lincoln.

mise of 1820, was unconstitutional and, therefore, null and void from its beginning; and that slaveholders had the right to take their slaves with them into any State or Territory of the Union, the same as horses and cattle, without impairing their rights thereto. And now, with this encouragement, the slave power bent all its energies to make slavery a national institution. On the other hand the power of Freedom had been so thoroughly aroused by the course of events and the aggressiveness of the slave power, that it exerted all its power to preserve the rights of freedom under the Declaration and the Constitution.

In speaking of this struggle, William H. Seward[15] of New York said, in the United States Senate, 1854: "Come on, then, gentlemen of the slave States; since there is no escaping your challenge,

[15]William H. Seward was born in Florida, N. Y., May 16, 1801. Became eminent as a lawyer, statesman, and diplomat. Was elected Governor of New York, 1838; re-elected, 1840. Elected U. S. Senator, 1849; re-elected, 1855. Appointed Secretary of State by President Lincoln, immediately after his first inauguration. He filled that important office with great ability until after the close of the Civil War. Died October 10, 1872.

Mr. Seward boldly denounced the slave power, and was an ardent defender of Freedom. He originated the two famous phrases, "the higher law" and "the irrepressible conflict." They were denounced by the advocates of slavery, but were caught up as the symbols of the political faith of the advocates of freedom.

He used the phrase "the higher law" in a speech delivered in the Senate, March 11, 1850, upon the admission of California into the Union. He said in part: "The Constitution devotes the domain to union, to justice, to defense, to welfare, and to liberty. But there is a 'higher law' than the Constitution, which regulates our authority over the domain, and devotes it to the same noble purposes."

The phrase "irrepressible conflict" is found in a speech delivered at Rochester, N. Y., October 25, 1858, in the following connection: "It is an irrepressible conflict between opposing and enduring forces. It means that the United States must and will, sooner or later, become entirely a slaveholding nation or entirely a free labor nation. Either the cotton and rice fields of South Carolina and the sugar plantations of Louisiana will be ultimately tilled by free labor, and Charleston and New Orleans become marts for legitimate merchandise alone, or else the rye-fields and wheat-fields of Massachusetts and New York must again be surrendered by their farmers to slave culture and to the production of slaves, and Boston and New York become once more markets for trade in the bodies and souls of men."

I accept it on behalf of Freedom. We will engage in competition for the virgin soil of Kansas, and God give the victory to the side that is stronger in numbers as it is in right."

The slaveholders soon began to realize that when the power of Freedom exerted all its strength, that the power of Slavery in the Nation, to extend itself, was gone. They began to see the handwriting on the wall,—"Thou hast been weighed in the balance and found wanting." They began to see power departing from them, and declared, in effect, "If we cannot get what we want in the Union we will leave it and build a nation of our own; for power we must have." This, however, they had threatened for many years. But soon they determined to carry out their threats.

They were willing to sacrifice the Republic rather than lose their power. Rhett, of South Carolina, avowed that "the South must control the government or must fall." If our rights, as he assumed them to be, "are overthrown, let this be the last contest between the North and the South, and the long, weary night of our dishonor and humiliation be dispersed at last by the glorious dayspring of a Southern Confederacy."

The slave power now boldly advocated the re-opening of the slave trade, although that trade is declared by law to be piracy. They denounced the opposition to that trade as "the sickly sentiment of pretended philanthropy and diseased mental aberration of 'higher law fanatics'."

Jefferson Davis, in an address, in the autumn
of 1859, denounced the law of 1820, which declares
the slave trade to be piracy; and said that nothing
could "justify the government in branding as infamous the source from which the chief part of
the laboring population of the South is derived."
He also declared that "servitude" was essential
for the good of the black race; that slavery ought
to be protected by law in the territories; that Cuba
should be secured as being important for the interests of a Southern Confederacy; and that the
Union should be dissolved, if the republicans elected their candidate on the platform of putting a
stop to the further extension of slavery.[16]

What a vast power Freedom had to contend
against! — A great slave oligarchy, based on four
million slaves, valued at about two billion dollars,
knit together in interest for the promotion of its
power; and the tentacles of that power reaching
far out into states and nations. That oligarchy
had Freedom by the throat, trying to throttle it.
The great question then was, Would Freedom be
able to shake it off and crush it?

---

[16]Duyckinck's "History of the World," Vol. 4, p. 232.

CHAPTER IV.

CONSPIRACY AND SECESSION.

The great struggle between Freedom and Slavery, in Kansas, continued until finally Freedom was victorious, after a conflict—amounting to civil war, at times,—of five years or more. The slaveholding aristocracy was now more desperate than ever. The slaveholders had now come to the point where they saw that slavery would not be extended; that their power, once so great, was departing.

When, therefore, in 1860, the elements composing the Democracy split on the slavery question and Abraham Lincoln was elected President, and thereby the South lost power, the slaveholding aristocracy made the election of Mr. Lincoln the pretext for conspiring against and attempting to destroy the Union. Before the election Southern men threatened that in the event of the election of Mr. Lincoln the South would disrupt the Union. The Governor of South Carolina just the day before his election formally recommended secession to the Legislature of that State "in event of Abraham Lincoln's election to the presidency." Soon after his election the United States Senators and Federal office holders for that State resigned their places. There was a general feeling among most of the leaders in the South that in case Mr. Lincoln was elected, secession would and ought to take place; and so immediately thereafter prep-

arations were made in that direction, and a conspiracy formed to destroy the Union.

Secession was talked openly, even in the halls
of Congress. Senator Iverson, of Georgia, rose
in his seat in the Senate of the United States,[17]
and, with cool defiance, said: "We intend, Mr.
President, to go out peaceably if we can, forcibly
if we must; but I do not believe, with the Senator
from New Hampshire (Mr. Hale), that there is
going to be any war. If five or eight States go out,
they will necessarily draw all the other Southern
States after them. That is a consequence that
nothing can prevent. If five or eight States go
out of this Union, I should like to see the man
who would propose a declaration of war against
them, or attempt to force them into obedience to
the Federal Government at the point of the bayo-
net or the sword. If one State alone was to go
out, unsustained by her sister States, possibly war
might ensue, and there might be an attempt made
to coerce her, and that would give rise to civil
war; but, sir, South Carolina is not to go out
alone. In my opinion, she will be sustained by
all her Southern sisters. They may not all go out
immediately, but they will, in the end, join South
Carolina in this important movement; and we
shall, in the next twelve months, have a confederacy of the Southern States, and a government
inaugurated and in successful operation, which,
in my opinion, will be a government of the greatest prosperity and power the world has ever seen."

[17]December 5, 1860.

History records that early in January, 1861, while only South Carolina had actually seceded from the Union, though other Southern States had called conventions to consider the question, the United States Senators of the seven slave States farthest south practically assumed control of the whole movement, and their energy and unswerving singleness of purpose, aided by the telegraph, secured a rapidity of execution to which no other very extensive conspiracy of history can afford a parallel. The cardinal object of these Senators was to hurry the formation of a new national government, as an organized political reality which would rally the outright secessionists, claim the allegiance of the doubtful, and coerce those who still remained recalcitrant. At the head of this senatorial conspiracy, and of its executive committee, was Jefferson Davis,[18] Senator from Mississippi, and naturally the first official step toward the formation of a new government came from the Mississippi Legislature, where a committee reported, January 19th, 1861, resolutions in favor of a congress of delegates from the seceding States to provide for a Southern Confederacy. The other seceding States at once accepted the proposal, through their State conventions, which also ap-

[18]Jefferson Davis was born in Kentucky, 1808; but brought up in Mississippi, of which State his father, a planter and a Revolutionary officer, became a resident while it was a Territory. Graduate United States Military Academy, 1828. Was colonel of a regiment in the Mexican War. Appointed United States Senator by the Governor of Mississippi, in 1847; twice re-elected to the same position. Appointed Secretary of War by President Pierce in 1853. Went back into the United States Senate at the close of Pierce's administration, where he remained until he left it to become President of the Southern Confederacy in February, 1861. Died, 1889.

7

pointed the delegates on the ground that the people had entrusted the State conventions with unlimited powers. These delegates[19] met at Montgomery, Alabama, and, on the 8th day of February, 1861, organized the Southern Confederacy.

Thus organized, they, and others, bent all their energies, from this time on, to induce the remaining eight slave States to secede from the Union and join the Confederacy. In this, however, they were only partially successful.[20]

There was one notable exception to the idea that the South ought to withdraw from the Union in case Mr. Lincoln was elected.

Alexander H. Stephens,[21] one of the ablest men of Georgia, was opposed to it. In a speech delivered November 14, 1860, in the Hall of the House of Representatives of Georgia, at the request of members of the Legislature, he said in part: "The

[19]From the States of South Carolina, Georgia, Mississippi, Alabama, Florida, Louisiana, and Texas.

[20]Four more slave States joined the Confederacy soon after the firing on Fort Sumter, April 12, 1861, namely: Arkansas, North Carolina, Tennessee and Virginia—except West Virginia. The remaining four slave States—Delaware, Maryland, Kentucky, and Missouri—did not secede.

[21]Alexander H. Stephens was born in Taliaferro County, Georgia, February 11, 1812. Educated at Franklin College, by the aid of kind friends attracted to him by the quickness of his parts; graduated, 1832. Admitted to the bar and practiced his profession with great success. From 1837 to 1842 he was a member of the Georgia Legislature, and in 1848 he was elected to the lower House of Congress as a candidate of the old Whig party; but when that party went down he took refuge in the Union wing of Southern Democracy. He soon attained distinction in Congress as a sound thinker, and a skillful and eloquent debater. It was as lawyer, legislator, and orator that he won his reputation. The cast of his mind was deliberative and argumentative. He had but little executive ability, or power to lead men into action. He was the antithesis of Jefferson Davis. Stephens was elected Vice-President of the Southern Confederacy because the uncompromising secessionists thought, by placing him in that position, he would attract to the new government the men of moderate views, who were still attached to the Union. After the close of the Civil War he re-entered Congress, 1872. Author of two works on the Civil War. Died March 4, 1883.

first question that presents itself is, Shall the people of the South secede from the Union in consequence of the election of Mr. Lincoln to the presidency of the United States? In my judgment, the election of no man, constitutionally chosen to that high office, is sufficient cause for any State to separate from the Union. It ought to stand by and aid still in maintaining the Constitution of the country. To make a point of resistance to the Government, to withdraw from it because a man has been constitutionally elected, puts us in the wrong. We are pledged to maintain the Constitution. Many of us have sworn to support it. Can we, therefore, for the mere election of a man to the presidency, and that, too, in accordance with the prescribed forms of the Constitution, make a point of resistance to the Government, withdraw ourselves from it, without becoming the breakers of that sacred instrument ourselves? Would we not be in the wrong? Whatever fate is to befall this country, let it never be laid to the charge of the people of the South, and especially to the people of Georgia, that we are untrue to our national engagements. Let the fault and the wrong rest upon others. If all our hopes are to be blasted, if the Republic is to go down, let us be found to the last moment standing on the deck, with the Constitution of the United States waving over our heads. Let the fanatics of the North break the Constitution, if such is their fell purpose. Let the responsibility be upon them. But let not the South, let us not be the ones to commit the aggres-

sion. We went into the election with this people.
The result was different from what we wished;
but the election has been constitutionally held.
Were we to make a point of resistance to the Government and go out of the Union on that account,
the record would be made up hereafter against us.
* * * That this government of our fathers,
with all its defects, comes nearer the objects of all
good governments than any other on the face of
the earth, is my settled conviction. * * *
Where will you go, following the sun in his circuit
round the globe, to find a government that better
protects the liberties of the people and secures to
them the blessings that we enjoy? I think that
one of the evils that besets us is a surfeit of liberty,
an exuberance of the priceless blessings for which
we are ungrateful. * * * Have we not at the
South as well as the North grown great and happy
under its operation? Has any part of the world
ever shown such rapid progress in the development of wealth, and all the material resources of
power and greatness, as the Southern States have
under the general government?"

How prophetic the words, "the record would
be made up hereafter against us." Indeed, the
record has been made up against them.

The same opinions were reiterated by Mr. Stephens at the Georgia Secession Convention held
in January, 1861, less than a month before he
accepted the vice-presidency of the Confederacy
whose formation he had persistently opposed. In
this speech he said: "This step (of secession) once

taken can never be recalled; and all the baleful
and withering consequences that must follow, will
rest on the Convention for all coming time. When
we and our posterity shall see our lovely South
desolated by the demon of war, which this act of
yours will inevitably invite and call forth; when
our green fields of waving harvest shall be trod-
den down by the murderous soldiery and fiery
car of war sweeping over our land; our temples
of justice laid in ashes; all the horrors and
desolations of war upon us; who but this Convention will be held responsible for it? And who
but him who shall have given his vote for this
unwise and illtimed measure, as I honestly think
and believe, shall be held to strict account for
this suicidal act by the present generation, and
probably cursed and execrated by posterity for
all coming time, for the wide and desolating ruin
that will inevitably follow this act you now propose to perpetrate? Pause, I entreat you, and
consider for a moment what reasons you can give
that will ever satisfy yourselves in calmer mo-
ments—what reasons you can give to your fellow
sufferers in the calamity that it will bring upon
us. What reasons can you give to the nations
of the earth to justify it? They will be the calm
and deliberate judges in the case; and what cause
or one overt act can you name or point on which
to rest the plea of justification? What right has
the North assailed? What interest of the South
has been invaded? What justice has been denied?
and what claim founded in justice and right has

been withheld? Can either of you to-day name
one governmental act of wrong, deliberately and
purposely done by the government of Washington,
of which the South has a right to complain? I
challenge the answer. While on the other hand
let me show the facts (and believe me, gentlemen,
I am not here the advocate of the North; but I
am here the friend, the firm friend, and lover of
the South and her institutions, and for this reason
I speak thus plainly and faithfully for yours,
mine, and every other man's interest, the words
of truth and soberness), of which I wish you to
judge, and I will only state facts which are clear
and undeniable, and which now stand as records
authentic in the history of our country. When we
of the South demanded the slave-trade, or the importation of Africans for the cultivation of our
lands, did they not yield the right for twenty
years?[22] When we asked a three-fifth representation in Congress for our slaves, was it not granted?[23] When we asked and demanded the return
of any fugitive from justice, or the recovery of
those persons owing labor or allegiance, was it
not incorporated in the Constitution,[24] and again
ratified and strengthened by the Fugitive Slave
Law of 1850? But do you reply that in many
instances they have violated this compact, and
have not been faithful to their engagements? As
individuals and local communities, they may have
done so; but not by the sanction of the Govern-

---

[22]See Section 9, Article I, of the Constitution.
[23]See Section 2, Article I, of the Constitution.
[24]See Section 2, Article IV, of the Constitution.

ment; for that has always been true to Southern interests. Again, gentlemen, look at another act; when we have asked that more territory should be added, that we might spread the institution of slavery, have they not yielded to our demands in giving us Louisiana, Florida, and Texas, out of which four States have been carved, and ample territory for four more to be added in time, if you by this unwise and impolitic act do not destroy this hope, and perhaps, by it lose all, and have your last slave wrenched from you by stern military rule, as South America and Mexico were; or by the vindictive decree of a universal emancipation which may reasonably be expected to follow?

"But again, gentlemen, what have we to gain by this proposed change of our relation to the General Government? We have always had control of it, and can yet, if we remain in it, and are as united as we have been. We have had a majority of the Presidents chosen from the South; as well as the control and management of most of those chosen from the North. We have had sixty years of Southern Presidents to their twenty-four, thus controlling the Executive department. So of the Judges of the Supreme Court, we have had eighteen from the South and but eleven from the North; although nearly four-fifths of the judicial business has arisen in the Free States, yet a majority of the Court has always been from the South. This we have required so as to guard against any interpretation of the Constitution unfavorable to us. In like manner we have been

equally watchful to guard our interests in the
Legislative branch of Government. In choosing
the presiding Presidents (pro tem.) of the Senate,
we have had twenty-four to their eleven. Speakers
of the House we have had twenty-three, and they
twelve. While the majority of the Representatives, from their greater population, have always
been from the North, yet we have so generally
secured the Speaker, because he, to a great extent,
shapes and controls the legislation of the country.
Nor have we had less control in every other department of the General Government. Attorney
Generals we have had fourteen, while the North
have had but five. Foreign ministers we have had
eighty-six, and they but fifty-four. While three-
fourths of the business which demands diplomatic
agents abroad is clearly from the Free States,
from their greater commercial interest, yet we
have had the principal embassies so as to secure
the world markets for our cotton, tobacco, and
sugar on the best possible terms. We have had a
vast majority of the higher officers of both army
and navy, while a larger proportion of the soldiers
and sailors were drawn from the North. Equally
so of Clerks, Auditors, and Comptrollers filling the
executive department, the records show for the
last fifty years that of the three thousand thus
employed, we have had more than two-thirds of
the same, while we have but one-third of the white
population of the Republic.

"Again, look at another item, and one, be assured, in which we have a great and vital interest;

it is that of revenue, or means of supporting Government. From official documents, we learn that a fraction over three-fourths of the revenue collected for the support of the Government has uniformly been raised from the North.

"Pause now, while you can, gentlemen, and contemplate carefully and candidly these important items. Look at another necessary branch of Government. I mean the mail and postoffice privileges. The expense for the transportation of the mail in the Free States was, by the report of the Postmaster General for the year 1860, a little over $13,000,000, while the income was $19,000,000. But in the Slave States the transportation of the mail was $14,716,000, while the revenue from the same was $8,001,026, leaving a deficit of $6,704,974, to be supplied by the North for our accommodation, and without it we must have been entirely cut off from this most essential branch of Government.

"Leaving out of view, for the present, the countless millions of dollars you must expend in a war with the North, with tens of thousands of your sons and brothers slain in battle, and offered up as sacrifices upon the altar of your ambition—and for what, we ask again? Is it for the overthrow of the American Government, established by our common ancestry, cemented and built up by their sweat and blood, and founded on the broad principles of Right, Justice and Humanity? And, as such, I must declare here, as I have often done before, and which has been repeated by the great-

est and wisest statesmen and patriots in this and
other lands, that it is the best and freest Government—the most equal in its rights, the most
just in its decisions, the most lenient in its measures, and the most aspiring in its principles to
elevate the race of man, that the sun of heaven
ever shone upon. Now, for you to attempt to overthrow such a government as this, under which we
have lived for more than three-quarters of a century—in which we have gained our wealth, our
standing as a nation, our domestic safety while
the elements of peril are around us, with peace
and tranquillity accompanied with unbounded
prosperity and rights unassailed—is the height
of madness, folly, and wickedness, to which I can
neither lend my sanction nor my vote."

No man, in the South, so clearly understood
the situation as Mr. Stephens. His words were
prophetic.

Although he was a slaveholder, and a firm believer in slavery, yet he was a strong friend of
the Union and felt that it was no light matter
to sever that Union. His birth and early training
had much to do with this friendship for the Union.
He represented the conservative Union men of
the South.

He was born of humble parents and reared in
comparative poverty. By his own inherent powers
he had raised himself to the rank of a statesman,
and no man stood higher in the South than he—
with the great mass of the people. It may be truly
said that he represented the common people and

was the great "Commoner" of the South, as Thaddeus Stevens was of the North.

But he was overpowered in his views by the aristocracy of his State,—by menaces and in other ways,—by such men as Toombs,[25] Cobb, and others who were determined, right or wrong, to overthrow the Republic; and finally, he gave in his adhesion to the Confederacy and became its Vice-President.

In contrast with Mr. Stephens, I now refer to the typical aristocrat of the South—Jefferson Davis, of Mississippi, then a member of the Senate of the United States from that State. In January, 1861, he arose in his seat and addressed the Senate and said: "I rise, Mr. President, for the purpose of announcing to the Senate that I have satisfactory evidence that the State of Mississippi, by a solemn ordinance of her people in convention assembled, has declared her separation from the United States. Under these circumstances, of course, my functions are terminated here. * * * The occasion does not invite me to go into argument. * * * And yet it seems to become me to say something on the part of the State I here represent, on an occasion so solemn as this. It is known to Senators who have served with me here, that I have for many years advocated as an

---

[25]Robert Toombs, born in Washington, Georgia, 1810. Graduate Union College, New York, 1828. Admitted to the bar, 1830. Served in the Georgia Legislature; in Congress from 1844 to 1853, when he was elected United States Senator, retiring on secession of Georgia. He was a Southern fire-eater of a pronounced type, and an uncompromising Secessionist. Became Secretary of State of Southern Confederacy, and Brigadier General. Never accepted the general amnesty offered by the Government of the United States to the rebels at the close of Civil War. Died December 15, 1885.

essential attribute of State sovereignty, the right
of a State to secede from the Union. Therefore,
if I had not believed there was justifiable cause;
if I had thought that Mississippi was acting without sufficient provocation, or without any existing
necessity, I should still, under my theory of the
Government, because of my allegiance to the State
of which I am a citizen, have been bound by her
action. I, however, may be permitted to say that
I do think she has justifiable cause and I approve
of her act. I conferred with her people before that
act was taken, counseled them then that if the
state of things which they apprehended should
exist when the convention met, they should take
the action they have now adopted. * * * I
therefore say I concur in the action of the people
of Mississippi, believing it to be necessary and
proper, and should have been bound by their action
if my belief had been otherwise. * * * A
State finding herself in the condition in which
Mississippi has judged she is; in which her safety
requires that she should provide for the maintenance of her rights out of the Union, surrenders
all the benefits (and they are known to be many),
deprives herself of the advantages (they are known
to be great), severs all the ties of affection (and
they are close and enduring) which have bound her
to the Union; and thus divesting herself of every
benefit, taking upon herself every burden, she
claims to be exempt from any power to execute the
laws of the United States within her limits.   *   *

"It has been a conviction of pressing necessity,

it has been a belief that we are to be deprived in the Union, of the rights which our fathers bequeathed to us, which has brought Mississippi into her present decision. She has heard proclaimed the theory that all men are created free and equal, and this made the basis of an attack on her social institutions; and the sacred Declaration of Independence has been invoked to maintain the position of the equality of the races. * * * When our Constitution was formed, they were not put upon the footing of equality with white men—not even upon that of paupers and convicts, but so far as representation was concerned, were discriminated against as a lower caste only to be represented in a numerical proportion of three-fifths.

"Then, Senators, we recur to the compact which binds us together; we recur to the principles upon which our government was founded; and when you deny them, and when you deny to us, the right to withdraw from a government which thus prevented, threatens to be destructive of our rights, we but tread in the path of our fathers when we proclaim our independence, and take the hazard. This is done not in hostility to others, not to injure any section of the country, not even for our own pecuniary benefit, but from the high and solemn motive of defending and protecting the rights we inherited, and which it is our sacred duty to transmit unshorn to our children.

"I find in myself, perhaps, a type of the general feeling of my constituents towards yours. I am sure I feel no hostility to you, Senators of the

North. * * * I therefore feel that I but express their desire when I say I hope, and they hope for peaceful relations with you, though we must part. They may be mutually beneficial to us in the future as they have been in the past, if you so will it. The reverse may bring disaster on every portion of the country; and if you will have it thus, we will invoke the God of our fathers, who delivered them from the power of the lion, to protect us from the ravages of the bear, and thus, putting our trust in God, and to our firm hearts and strong arms we will vindicate the right as best we may.

"Mr. President and Senators, having made the announcement which the occasion seemed to me to require, it only remains for me to bid you a final adieu."

What a spectacle was here presented! A Senator of the United States, who had taken an oath to support its Constitution, rising in his place and solemnly declaring that he had counseled the disruption of his country; and that whether he thought there was cause or no cause for his State withdrawing from the Union he would stand by her,—under the false claim that his allegiance to her was paramount to that of the Union.

I think of but one parallel in history with this base betrayal of country; and that is Catiline, a member of the Roman Senate, who formed and headed a conspiracy to destroy his country. Like Catiline, Davis conspired to destroy his country

while he yet was in the Senate. But there was
no Cicero[26] there to denounce him.

CHAPTER V.

THE SOUTHERN CONFEDERACY.

The conspiracy was carried out by the leaders
of the South, of which Mr. Davis was chief, eleven
States seceding from the Union[27] and forming a
Confederacy, with a written Constitution, under
the name of "The Confederate States of America,"
and chose Jefferson Davis of Mississippi, as their
President, and Alexander H. Stephens of Georgia,
as their Vice President—the two representative
types of the people of the South.

The records of history show that the politicians
of South Carolina, according to agreement, took
the first step toward open rebellion. For that purpose, an extraordinary session of the Legislature
was held at the time of the Presidential election,
Nov. 6, 1860, and, soon after the result was known,

[26]Marcus Tullius Cicero, the greatest orator of Rome, and one of
the most illustrious of her statesmen, was born at Arpinum, on the
3d of January, in the year 106 B. C. Cicero, while consul (63 B. C.),
frustrated the conspiracy of Catiline with great skill and promptness. The history of this conspiracy is given by Sallust, the great
Roman historian, in a remarkably clear, concise and nervous style.
His account of it, however, does not do justice to Cicero.

[27]These were the following States, named in the order of their
passing secession ordinances: South Carolina, December 20, 1860;
Mississippi, January 9, 1861; Florida, January 10; Alabama, January
11; Georgia, January 19; Louisiana, January 26; Texas, February
1; Virginia, April 17; Arkansas, May 6; North Carolina, May
20; Tennessee, June 8. The first seven seceded before and the
remaining four after the firing on Fort Sumter, April 12, 1861. The
Confederacy was formed by the first seven on the 8th of February,
1860, at Montgomery, Alabama; the others joined it as soon as they
passed ordinances of secession, although as a matter of fact many
of the leaders in these States had been acting with it before that.

the Legislature authorized a convention of delegates, for the purpose of declaring the State sep-
arated from the Union, and taking measures for
maintaining what they called the "Sovereignty of
South Carolina." The members of that Convention
were chosen on the 3d of December, and they met
at Charleston. On the 20th day of December, 1860,
they adopted an Ordinance of Secession;[28] and
that evening, in the presence of the Governor and
his council, the Legislature, and a vast concourse
of citizens, it was signed in the great Hall of
the South Carolina Institute, by one hundred and
seventy of the members.

On this historic occasion, a significant banner
was hung back of the chair of the president of the
convention. Upon it was represented an arch
composed of fifteen stars (each indicating a slave-
labor State) rising out of a heap of broken and
disordered stones, representing the Free-labor
States. The key-stone was South Carolina, on
which stood a statue of John C. Calhoun. This
banner was a declaration of the intention of the
convention to destroy the Republic, and to erect
upon its ruins an empire whose corner-stone should
be slavery. Beneath the design on the banner
were the words: "Built from the Ruins."[29]

---

[28]This ordinance of secession reads as follows: "We, the people
of South Carolina, in convention assembled, do declare and ordain,
and it is hereby declared and ordained, that the ordinance adopted
by us in convention, on the twenty-third day of May, in the year
of our Lord one thousand seven hundred and eighty-eight, whereby
the Constitution of the United States was ratified, and also all Acts
and parts of Acts of the General Assembly of the State, ratifying
Amendments of the said Constitution, are hereby repealed, and the
union now subsisting between South Carolina and other States,
under the name of the United States of America, is hereby dissolved."

[29]Lossing's "The First Century of the United States."

This action of South Carolina was speedily imitated by the politicians, in the interest of the conspirators, in the other States which seceded from the Union.

Mr. Stephens, now launched on the sea of rebellion, undertook to vindicate this new Government and its Constitution, in a speech delivered at Savannah, Georgia, on the 21st day of March, 1861, which is all that need be said of them; for his attempted vindication, in the light of the truth, is their condemnation.

"The new Constitution," said Mr. Stephens, "has put at rest forever all the agitating questions relating to our peculiar institutions—African slavery as it exists among us—the proper status of the negro in our form of civilization. This was the immediate cause of the late rupture and present revolution. Jefferson, in his forecast, had anticipated this as the 'rock upon which the old Union would split.' He was right. What was conjecture with him, is now a realized fact. But whether he fully comprehended the great truth upon which that rock stood and stands, may be doubted. The prevailing ideas entertained by him and most of the leading statesmen at the time of the formation of the old Constitution (Constitution of the United States), were that the enslavement of the African was in violation of the laws of nature; that it was wrong in principle, socially, morally, and politically. It was an evil they knew not well how to deal with, but the general opinion of the men of that day was, that somehow or other, in the order

8

of Providence, the institution would be evanescent
and pass away. This idea, though not incorporated in the Constitution, was the prevailing idea
at the time. The Constitution, it is true, secured
every essential guarantee to the institution while
it should last, and hence no argument can be justly
used against the constitutional guarantees thus
secured, because of the common sentiment of the
day. Those ideas, however, were fundamentally
wrong. They rested upon the assumption of the
equality of races. This was an error. It was
a sandy foundation, and the idea of a government
built upon it; when the 'storm came and the wind
blew, it fell.'

"Our new Government is founded upon exactly
the opposite idea; its foundations are laid, its
corner-stone rests upon the great truth that the
negro is not equal to the white man. That slavery
—subordination to the superior race, is his natural
and normal condition. This, our new Government,
is the first, in the history of the world, based upon
this great physical and moral truth. This truth
has been slow in the process of its development,
like all other truths in the various departments of
science. It has been so even amongst us. Many
who hear me, perhaps, can recollect well, that
this truth was not generally admitted, even within
their day. The errors of the past generation still
clung to many as late as twenty years ago. Those
at the North who still cling to these errors, with
a zeal above knowledge, we justly denominate
fanatics. * * *

"It is the first government ever instituted upon principles of strict conformity to nature, and the ordination of Providence, in furnishing the materials of human society. Many governments have been founded upon the principle of certain classes; but the classes thus enslaved, were of the same race, and in violation of the laws of nature. Our system commits no such violation of nature's laws. The negro, by nature, or by the curse against Canaan, is fitted for that condition which he occupies in our system. The architect, in the construction of buildings, lays the foundation with the proper materials, the granite; then comes the brick or the marble. The substratum of our society is made of the material fitted by nature for it, and by experience we know that it is best, not only for the superior, but for the inferior race that it should be so. It is, indeed, in conformity with the ordinance of the Creator. It is not for us to inquire into the wisdom of His ordinances, or to question them. For His own purposes He has made one race to differ from another, as He has made 'one star to differ from another star in glory.'

"The great objects of humanity are best attained when conformed to His laws and decrees, in the formation of governments, as well as in all things else. Our Confederacy is founded upon principles in strict conformity with these laws. This stone which was first rejected by the first builders 'is become the chief stone of the corner' in our new edifice.

"The progress of disintegration in the old

Union may be expected to go on with almost absolute certainty. We are now the nucleus of a grow-
ing power, which, if we are true to ourselves, our
destiny, and high mission, will become the controlling power on this continent. To what extent
accessions will go on in the process of time, or
where it will end, the future will determine."

CHAPTER VI.

BUCHANAN AND THE REBELLION.

From the time of the election of Mr. Lincoln,
the conspirators used every effort to cripple the
Government; and many of them held high positions in the Government, so that they were in a
position to carry out their treasonable designs.

President Buchanan[30] did nothing to foil the
conspirators, some of whom were in his cabinet;
neither did he make any effort to prevent a disruption of the Union, nor but little to protect the

[30]James Buchanan was born in Franklin County, Pennsylvania,
April 23, 1791. Educated at Dickenson College, where he graduated
at the age of eighteen. In 1809 he was admitted to the bar, and
was soon in successful practice. In 1814, when only twenty-three
years of age, he was elected to a seat in the Legislature of Pennsylvania. This was his first prominent appearance in public life.
In 1815 he distinguished himself in his State Leg.slature as an opponent of the United States Bank, and became one of the foremost men in the Democratic party. Elected to Congress in 1820, and
there soon became distinguished as a speaker and debater. After
ten years' service, he retired from Congress in 1831 when President
Jackson appointed him Minister to Russia. In 1833 he was elected
to the United States Senate, where he served ten years. President
Polk called him to his cabinet, as Secretary of State; and in 1849
he again retired to private life. In 1853 he was appointed Minister
to England. In November, 1856, he was elected President of the
United States by the Democratic party, and was inaugurated as
such March 4th, 1857. At the close of his term, March 4th, 1861, he
retired to private life at his country seat, called "Wheatland," near
Lancaster, Pennsylvania, where he died June 1, 1868.

property of the United States in the rebellious
States; claiming that he did not have the power
to do so.

The conspirators,—who had been colleagues or
were disciples of John C. Calhoun,—had been for
years plotting treason against the Government of
the United States. They were of one mind in regard to the overt act; but they differed somewhat
as to time and manner. Those of South Carolina
who, by common sentiment, were expected to lead
in the great movement, were anxious for immediate action, and when they found those of other
sister slave-States hesitating, they resolved not
to wait for their co-operation. For a while this
question divided the secessionists, but it was soon
settled by general co-operation. Everything was
favorable to their plans. Three, if not four, of the
leading conspirators were then members of President Buchanan's cabinet, and the President himself and his Attorney General (Jeremiah S. Black,[31]
of Pennsylvania) were ready to declare, and did
declare, that the Constitution gave the President
of the United States no power to stay the arm
of rebellion against the Government. Of the President, Jacob Thompson,[32] of his cabinet, said:
"Buchanan is the truest friend of the South I have
ever known in the North. He is a jewel of a
man."[33]

---

[31]Jeremiah S. Black was born in Pennsylvania, 1810. Attorney
General under President Buchanan. In December, 1860, appointed
Secretary of State by the President in place of Gen. Cass, resigned.
Died, 1883.
[32]Jacob Thompson was born in North Carolina, 1810. Secretary
of the Interior under President Buchanan from March, 1857, to January 7, 1861. Was one of the most active secessionists before and
after the breaking out of the Civil War. Died, 1885.
[33]Autograph letter, November 20, 1860.

Howell Cobb of Georgia, Secretary of the Treasury, wished to hold back the blow until the close of Buchanan's term, but he was overruled by the other conspirators, who counted upon the President's passive, if not active, sympathy with them.[34]

During the four months intervening between the Presidential election, November 6, 1860, and the inauguration of Mr. Lincoln, March 4, 1861, those favoring secession in the South had practical control of their section, for while President Buchanan hesitated as to his constitutional powers and failed to perform his duty as the Executive of the Nation, the conspirators, who were in his cabinet and in the Senate, were aiding their Southern friends in every practical way.

These men, who had taken a solemn oath to support the Constitution of the United States, sat in their places in Washington, were paid by the Government of the United States to promote the best interests of that Government and of the Republic, and instead of doing that were plotting its destruction. They remained in their positions only for the purpose of insuring the success of their conspiracy—only that they might counterbalance the votes of men loyal to the Republic, and keep at dead lock all the essential functions of government. These are not mere assertions nor vague deductions with no evidence to support them. The evidence is abundant, but many of the histories of the day do not give it; neither do they refer to a conspiracy nor to the conspirators. The

[34]Lossing's "The First Century of the United States."

fact is, however, that the records of treacherous conspiracy show none more infamous.

Senator D. L. Yulee, of Florida, in a private letter to one of his constituents, Joseph Finegan, told the designs of the conspirators in Washington.[35] "On the other side," he said, "is a copy of resolutions adopted at a consultation of the Senators from the seceding States in which Georgia, Alabama, Louisiana, Arkansas, Texas, Mississippi and Florida, were present.

"The idea of the meeting was that the States should go out at once, and provide for the early organization of a Confederate government, not later than 15th February. This time is allowed to enable Louisiana and Texas to participate. It seemed to be the opinion that if we left here force, loan, and volunteer bills might be passed, which would put Mr. Lincoln in immediate condition for hostility; whereas if by remaining in our places until the 4th of March, it is thought we can keep the hands of Mr. Buchanan tied, and disable the Republicans from effecting any legislation which will strengthen the hands of the incoming administration.

"The resolutions will be sent by the delegation to the President of the convention. I have not been able to find Mr. Mallory[36] this morning. Hawkins is in Connecticut. I have therefore thought it best to send you this copy of the resolutions."

[35]Autograph letter dated at Washington, January 1, 1861.
[36]Stephen B. Mallory, a United States Senator from Florida, afterward made Secretary of the Navy of the Southern Confederacy.

To add to the shame and perfidy, this letter
was secured a swift and free passage to Mr. Finegan under the Honorable (?) writer's Senatorial
frank.[37]

With these men, says the historian of that
time, secession was a foregone conclusion, and delay and vacillation on the part of the half-hearted
supporters of the Government, in power, only
aided the accomplishment of their designs. This
was made plain on the 31st of December, 1860, by
Senator Benjamin,[38] of Louisiana, a State which
had not yet taken even the preliminary steps to
secession. In a speech meant both as a threat and
a valedictory, he announced to the Senate that
during the next week Mississippi, Alabama, and
Florida would separate from the Union; that a
week after Georgia would follow them, to be followed shortly by Louisiana and Arkansas. He declared that the day of adjustment was past, and
that when the members of that body parted, they
would part to meet again as Senators in one
common council-chamber of the Nation no
more forever; and, announcing it as his belief
that there could not be peaceable secession, he
defied the attempt to subdue the revolted people
to the authority of the Constitution. Couching
this defiance in the phraseology adopted by the
conspirators, he closed his speech with these
words:

[37] Harper's "Pictorial History of the Great Rebellion," pp. 31, 32.
[38] Judah P. Benjamin was born in St. Domingo, 1812. Removed to
New Orleans, La., 1831. United States Senator, 1852-1861. Appointed
Attorney General Southern Confederacy, 1861. At the close of the
Civil War went to England, where he practiced law, and became
a Q. C. Died, 1885.

"What may be the fate of this horrible contest none can foretell; but this much I will say—the fortunes of war may be adverse to our arms; you may carry desolation into our peaceful land, and with torch and firebrand may set our cities in flames; you may even emulate the atrocities of those who in the days of our Revolution hounded on the bloodthirsty savage; you may give the protection of your advancing armies to the furious fanatics who desire nothing more than to add the horrors of servile insurrection to civil war; you may do this and more, but you never can subjugate us; you never can subjugate the free sons of the soil into vassals paying tribute to your power; you can never degrade them into a servile and inferior race—never, never, never!"[39]

On December 30th, 1860, in answer to the visiting commissioners from South Carolina, R. W. Barnwell, J. H. Adams, and James L. Orr, who formally submitted that State's Ordinance of Secession and demanded possession of the forts in Charleston harbor, President Buchanan said:

"In answer to this communication, I have to say that my position as President of the United States was clearly defined in the message to Congress on the 3d inst. In that I stated that 'apart from the execution of the laws, so far as this may be practicable, the Executive has no authority to decide what shall be the relations between the Federal Government and South Carolina. He has been invested with no such discretion. He possesses no

---

[39]Harper's "Pictorial History of the Great Rebellion," p. 32.

power to change the relations heretofore existing
between them, much less to acknowledge the independence of that State. This would be to invest
a mere executive officer with the power of recognizing the dissolution of the Confederacy among
our thirty-three sovereign States. It bears no re-
semblance to the recognition of a foreign de facto
government, involving no such responsibility.
Any attempt to do this would, on his part, be a
naked act of usurpation. It is, therefore, my duty
to submit to Congress the whole question in all its
bearings.'

"Such is my opinion still. I could, therefore,
meet you only as private gentlemen of the highest
character, and was entirely willing to communi-
cate to Congress any proposition you might have
to make to that body upon the subject. Of this
you were well aware. It was my earnest desire
that such a disposition might be made of the whole
subject by Congress, who alone possess the power,
as to prevent the inauguration of a civil war between the parties in regard to the possession of the
Federal forts in the harbor of Charleston."

President Buchanan, in his annual message of
December 3, 1860, had appealed to Congress to institute an amendment to the Constitution recognizing the rights of the Southern States in regard
to slavery in the Territories, and as this document
embraced the views which subsequently led to
such a general discussion of the right of secession
and of the right to coerce a State, I make a liberal
quotation from it:

"I have purposely confined my remarks to revolutionary resistance because it has been claimed within the last few years that any State, whenever this shall be its sovereign will and pleasure, may secede from the Union in accordance with the Constitution, and without any violation of the constitutional rights of the other members of the Confederacy. That as each became parties to the Union by the vote of its own people assembled in convention, so any one of them may retire from the Union in a similar manner by the vote of such a convention.

"In order to justify secession as a constitutional remedy, it must be on the principle that the Federal Government is a mere voluntary association of States, to be dissolved at pleasure by any one of the contracting parties. If this be so, the Confederacy is a rope of sand, to be penetrated and dissolved by the first adverse wave of public opinion in any of the States. In this manner our thirty-three States may resolve themselves into as many petty, jarring, and hostile republics, each one retiring from the Union without responsibility whenever any sudden excitement might impel them to such a course. By this process a Union might be entirely broken into fragments in a few weeks, which cost our forefathers many years of toil, privation, and blood to establish.

"Such a principle is wholly inconsistent with the history as well as the character of the Federal Constitution. After it was framed with the greatest deliberation and care, it was submitted to con-

ventions of the people of the several States for ratification. Its provisions were discussed at length
in these bodies, composed of the first men of the
country. Its opponents contended that it conferred powers upon the Federal Government dangerous to the rights of the States, whilst its advocates maintained that, under a fair construction
of the instrument, there was no foundation for
such apprehensions. In that mighty struggle between the first intellects of this or any other country, it never occurred to any individual, either
among its opponents or advocates, to assert or
even to intimate that their efforts were all vain
labor, because the moment that any State felt herself aggrieved she might secede from the Union.
What a crushing argument would this have
proved against those who dreaded that the rights
of the States would be endangered by the Constitution. The truth is, that it was not until some
years after the origin of the Federal Government
that such a proposition was first advanced. It
was afterwards met and refuted by the conclusive
arguments of General Jackson,[40] who, in his mes-

---

[40]Andrew Jackson was born March 15, 1767, in the Waxhaw settlement, Mecklenberg County, North Carolina, close to the South
Carolina boundary line. When but a lad he entered the revolutionary army and was taken prisoner by the British, where he
received brutal treatment. In 1784 he began the study of law in
Salisbury, North Carolina. Four years later he removed to Nashville, Tenn., where he opened a law office. In 1797 he was elected
United States Senator, but soon resigned. Re-elected in 1823.
During the war of 1812 Jackson was appointed major general in
the regular army, and gained a great victory over the British at
New Orleans. By this, and his victories over the Indians, he
acquired great popularity, and in consequence was elected President
of the United States by the Democratic party, in 1828; and again
in 1832.
He was a man of indomitable will and of great firmness; and
earned the nickname of "Old Hickory." It was while he was President that South Carolina undertook to nullify a law of Congress,
passed in 1828, in regard to the tariff—a protective tariff. John C.

sage of the 16th of January, 1833, transmitting the nullifying ordinance of South Carolina to Congress, employs the following language: 'The right of the people of a single State to absolve themselves at will and without the consent of the other States from their most solemn obligations, and hazard the liberty and happiness of the millions composing this Union, cannot be acknowledged. Such authority is believed to be utterly repugnant both to the principles upon which the General Government is constituted, and to the objects which it was expressly formed to attain.'

"It is not pretended that any clause in the Constitution gives countenance to such a theory. It is altogether founded upon inference, not from any language contained in the instrument itself, but from the sovereign character of the several States by which it was ratified. But it is beyond the power of a State, like an individual, to yield a portion of its sovereign rights to secure the remainder. In the language of Mr. Madison, who has been called the father of the Constitution, 'It was formed by the States—that is, by the people in each of the States acting in their highest sovereign capacity, and formed consequently by the same authority which formed the State constitutions.' 'Nor is the Government of the United

Calhoun and Robt. Y. Hayne were at the head of this movement. South Carolina said, in effect, "If the Government of the United States undertakes to enforce this law we will resist by arms and go out of the Union." Jackson replied, "No, you will not!" that "Our Federal Union must be preserved." The nullifiers got no sympathy from him; but his determined stand at that time did not prevent the same State from seceding from the Union thirty years later. Jackson died at his farm of the Hermitage, near Nashville, June 8, 1845.

States, created by the Constitution, less a Government, in the strict sense of the term within the
sphere of its powers, than the governments created by the constitutions of the States are within
their several spheres. It is like them organized
into legislative, executive, and judiciary departments. It operates, like them, directly on persons
and things; and, like them, it has at command a
physical force for executing the powers committed to it.'

"It was intended to be perpetual, and not to be
annulled at the pleasure of any one of the contracting parties. The old Articles of Confederation were entitled, 'Articles of Confederation and
Perpetual Union between the States'; and by the
thirteenth article it is expressly declared that 'the
articles of this Confederation shall be inviolably
observed by every State, and the Union shall be
perpetual.' The preamble to the Constitution of
the United States, having express reference to the
Articles of Confederation, recites that it was established 'in order to form a more perfect union.'
And yet it is contended that this 'more perfect
union' does not include the essential attribute of
perpetuity.

"But the Constitution has not only conferred
these high powers upon Congress, but it has adopted effectual means to restrain the States from interfering with their exercise. For that purpose
it has in strong prohibitory language expressly
declared[41] that 'no State shall enter into any

----

[41]See Section 10 of Article I, the Constitution.

treaty, alliance, or confederation; grant letters of marque and reprisal; coin money; emit bills of credit; make anything but gold and silver coin a tender in payment of debts; pass any bill of attainder, ex post facto law, or law impairing the obligation of contracts.' Moreover, 'without the consent of Congress no State shall lay any imposts or duties on any imports or exports, except what may be absolutely necessary for executing its inspection laws,' and if they exceed this amount, the excess shall belong to the United States. And 'no State shall, without the consent of Congress, lay any duty of tonnage, keep troops or ships of war in time of peace, enter into any agreement or compact with another State, or with a foreign power, or engage in war, unless actually invaded or in such imminent danger as will not admit of delay.'

"In order still further to secure the uninterrupted exercise of these high powers against State interposition, it is provided 'that this Constitution and the laws of the United States which shall be made in pursuance thereof, and all treaties made or which shall be made under the authority of the United States, shall be the supreme law of the land; and the judges in every State shall be bound thereby, anything in the Constitution or laws of any State to the contrary notwithstanding.'[42]

"The solemn sanction of religion has been superadded to the obligations of official duty, and all Senators and Representatives of the United States,

[42]See Article VI of the Constitution.

all members of State Legislatures, and all executive and judicial officers, 'both of the United States
and of the several States, shall be bound by oath
or affirmation to support this Constitution.'[43]

"In order to carry into effect these powers, the
Constitution has established a perfect Government in all its forms, legislative, executive, and
judicial; and this Government to the extent of its
powers acts directly upon the individual citizens
of every State, and executes its own decrees by the
agency of its own officers. In this respect it dif-
fers entirely from the Government under the old
confederation, which was confined to making
requisitions on the States in their sovereign character. This left it in the discretion of each
whether to obey or refuse, and they often declined
to comply with such requisitions. It thus became
necessary, for the purpose of removing this bar-
rier, and 'in order to form a more perfect union,'
to establish a Government which could act directly upon the people and execute its own laws
without the intermediate agency of the States.
This has been accomplished by the Constitution
of the United States. In short, the Government
created by the Constitution, and deriving its authority from the sovereign people of each of the
several States, has precisely the same right to exercise its power over the people of all these States
in the enumerated cases, that each one of them
possesses over subjects not delegated to the United

---

[43]See Article VI of the Constitution.

States, but 'reserved to the States respectively or to the people.'[44]

"To the extent of the delegated powers the Constitution of the United States is as much a part of the constitution of each State, and is as binding upon its people, as though it had been textually inserted therein.

"This Government, therefore, is a great and powerful Government, invested with all the attributes of sovereignty over the special subjects to which its authority extends. Its framers never intended to implant in its bosom the seeds of its own destruction nor were they at its creation guilty of the absurdity of providing for its own dissolution. It was not intended by its framers to be the baseless fabric of a vision, which, at the touch of the enchanter, would vanish into thin air, but a substantial and mighty fabric, capable of resisting the slow decay of time, and of defying the storms of ages. Indeed, well may the jealous patriots of that day have indulged fears that a Government of such high power might violate the reserved rights of the States, and wisely did they adopt the rule of a strict construction of these powers to prevent the danger. But they did not fear, nor had they any reason to imagine that the Constitution would ever be so interpreted as to enable any State by her own act, and without the consent of her sister States, to discharge her people from all or any of their federal obligations.

"It may be asked, then, are the people of the

44See Article X of Amendments to the Constitution.

9

States without redress against the tyranny and
oppression of the Federal Government? By no
means. The right of resistance on the part of the
governed against the oppression of their governments cannot be denied. It exists independently
of all constitutions, and has been exercised at all
periods of the world's history. Under it, old governments have been destroyed and new ones have
taken their place. It is embodied in strong and
express language in our own Declaration of Independence. But the distinction must ever be observed that this is revolution against an established government, and not a voluntary secession
from it by virtue of an inherent constitutional
right. In short, let us look the danger fairly in
the face; secession is neither more nor less than
revolution. It may or it may not be a justifiable
revolution; but still it is revolution."

The President having thus set forth his views
as to the Constitution, and having attempted to
demonstrate that there is no warrant in the Constitution for secession, but that this was inconsistent both with its letter and spirit, then defines
his own duties and powers, as the Executive head
of the Nation.

"What, in the meantime," he says, "is the responsibility and true position of the Executive?
He is bound by solemn oath, before God and the
country, 'to take care that the laws be faithfully
executed,' and from this obligation he cannot be
absolved by any human power. But what if the
performance of this duty, in whole or in part, has

been rendered impracticable by events over which he could have exercised no control? Such, at the present moment, is the case throughout the State of South Carolina, so far as the laws of the United States to secure the administration of justice by means of the Federal judiciary are concerned. All the Federal officers within its limits, through whose agency alone these laws can be carried into execution, have already resigned. We no longer have a district judge, a district attorney, or a marshal in South Carolina. In fact, the whole machinery of the Federal Government necessary for the distribution of remedial justice among the people has been demolished, and it would be difficult, if not impossible, to replace it.

"The only acts of Congress on the statute book bearing upon this subject are those of the 28th February, 1795, and 3rd March, 1807. These authorize the President, after he shall have ascertained that the marshal, with his posse comitatus, is unable to execute civil or criminal process in any particular case, to call forth the militia and employ the army and navy to aid him in performing this service, having first by proclamation commanded the insurgents 'to disperse and retire peaceably to their respective abodes within a limited time.' This duty cannot by possibility be performed in a State where no judicial authority exists to issue process, and where there is no marshal to execute it, and where, even if there were such an officer, the entire population would constitute one solid combination to resist him.

"The same insuperable obstacles do not lie in the way of executing the laws for the collection of customs. The revenue still continues to be collected, as heretofore, at the custom house in Charleston, and should the collector unfortunately resign, a successor may be appointed to perform this duty.

"Then, in regard to the property of the United States in South Carolina. This has been purchased for a fair equivalent, 'by the consent of the Legislature of the State,' 'for the erection of forts, magazines, arsenals,' etc., and over these the authority 'to exercise exclusive legislation' has been expressly granted by the Constitution to Congress.[45] It is not believed that any attempt will be made to expel the United States from this property by force; but if in this I should prove to be mistaken, the officer in command of the forts has received orders to act strictly on the defensive. In such a contingency the responsibility for consequences would rightfully rest upon the heads of the assailants."

Here the President sets forth the part of his message which he quoted in his answer to the Commissioners who presented to him the ordinance of secession of South Carolina;[46] and then goes on and gives his opinion that the Constitution of the United States has conferred no power on the Government to coerce a State to remain in the Union, in the following language:

---

[45]See Section 8 of Article I, the Constitution.
[46]See page 121, ante.

"The question fairly stated is, Has the Constitution delegated to Congress the power to coerce a State into submission which is attempting to withdraw, or has actually withdrawn from the Confederacy? If answered in the affirmative, it must be on the principle that the power has been conferred upon Congress to make war against a State.

"After much serious reflection, I have arrived at the conclusion that no such power has been delegated to Congress or to any other department of the Federal Government. It is manifest, upon an inspection of the Constitution, that this is not among the specific and enumerated powers granted to Congress; and it is equally apparent that its exercise is not 'necessary and proper for carrying into execution' any of these powers. * * *"

CHAPTER VII.

AN ARGUMENT.

The President's argument, against the claimed right of secession, was strong; but weak on the vital point—the remedy against those who were attempting to destroy the Union by secession. He clearly demonstrated that the Constitution was intended by its framers to be perpetual; that it did not provide for its own termination; that the Constitution was formed by the people acting in their highest sovereign capacity; and that the

Union made by that Constitution is not a mere
voluntary association of States, to be dissolved at
pleasure by any one of them, but that it is an everlasting Union to be dissolved only by the consent
of the sovereign power that made it—the people
of the United States. In the words of Washington, the president of the convention which framed
the Constitution, and the first President of the Republic under that Constitution, "Until changed by
an explicit and deliberate act of the whole people,
it is sacredly obligatory upon all." Charles C.
Pinckney[47] of South Carolina, another member of
the convention which framed the Constitution,
said, in the Legislature of South Carolina, just before the people of that State adopted the Constitution, "Let us, then, consider all attempts to
weaken this Union by maintaining that each State
is separately and individually independent, as a
species of political heresy which can never benefit
us, but may bring on us the most serious dis-
tresses."

However, if the Government of the United
States has no power to protect its own life—save
itself from destruction—then, indeed, is it "a rope
of sand, to be penetrated and dissolved by the first
adverse wave of public opinion in any of the
States." But this is a Government invested with

---

[47]Charles Cotesworth Pinckney was born in Charleston, S. C.,
February 25th, 1746. Educated in England. Began practice of law
in Charleston, 1769. Entered revolutionary army, and was captured
at the fall of Charleston. Appointed U. S. Minister to the French
Republic, 1796, and second major general in the United States army,
1797. Author of "Millions for defence, but not one cent for tribute."
He, aided by others of the South, who helped to frame the Constitution of the United States, 1787, compelled the concessions made
in the Constitution with slavery. Died August 16, 1825.

all the attributes of sovereignty; and its Constitution and the laws and treaties made thereunder, are the supreme law of the land.[48] "Its framers," says the President, "never intended to implant in its bosom the seeds of its own destruction, nor were they at its creation guilty of the absurdity of providing for its own dissolution. It was not intended by its framers to be the baseless fabric of a vision, which, at the touch of the enchanter, would vanish into thin air, but a substantial and mighty fabric, capable of resisting the slow decay of time, and of defying the storms of ages."

But this being true, does not the Government have the inherent power to save itself? When assailed by internal foes must it keep quiet and permit its own destruction? May it not be said that every government has the power to preserve itself whether it is so written or not? If the Government of the United States does not have this power, either in or outside of the Constitution, of preserving itself, then, indeed, it has "implanted in its bosom the seeds of its own destruction;" and is incapable of "defying the storms of ages." But is it true that the Constitution does not provide for the maintenance of the Government organized under it? It is the organic and fundamental law of the land, binding on all the States and all the people of the United States; and it provides that, "the United States shall guarantee to every State in this Union a republican form of government;"[49]

---

[48]See Article VI. of the Constitution.
[49]Section 4 of Article IV.

and that, " no State shall enter into any treaty, alliance, or confederation."[50]   These provisions are absolute in their terms; and no department of the National Government nor of the State governments, has the right to violate them.

The Government of the United States, and of the several States, are republican in form and must be maintained until a new form of government is adopted by all the people of the United States in their sovereign capacity as the source of all political power. It is the imperative duty, then, of the Government of the United States, under the Constitution, not to permit any State in the Union to establish any other form of government than it had when it became a member of the Union under that Constitution; nor to permit any State in the Union to "enter into any treaty, alliance, or confederation" with any other State. Indeed, any other doctrine might soon destroy the whole fabric of American free government. One State, for instance, might change its form of government to a limited monarchy; another to an absolute monarchy; and so on through all the different forms of government known to man. And, again, a State might enter into an "alliance, or confederation," with another State or States, either in or out of the Union. In this way causing the ruin of the whole fabric of republican government "which cost our forefathers so many years of toil, privation, and blood to establish."

These considerations being true, does it not fol-

[50]Section 10 of Article I.

low that the Government of the United States has the power to take all the necessary steps to prevent any such violations of the provisions of the Constitution? And that whenever any State undertakes to withdraw from the Union and establish a government of its own, or to enter into an "alliance, or confederation" with another State or States—as South Carolina and other States of the Union did and formed a Confederacy—does it not have the power to coerce that State back into the Union—back into the relations it occupied in our system of government before it took on its new relations? If this be not true, then, indeed, is the Constitution of none effect, and the Government under it weak, instead of "great and powerful."

But it is a great and powerful Government, having full power to enforce its Constitution and its laws. In the execution of these it is backed by the whole military power of the nation, and that power is under the control of the President as commander-in-chief. With that power to sustain him in executing the mandates of the Constitution, and the laws enacted under it, the President of the United States can overthrow all its enemies —internal and external—when he acts with promptness and energy. If the time should ever come, however, when this is not true the days of the Republic are numbered.

CHAPTER VIII.

BUCHANAN AND DAVIS.

At the time President Buchanan sent his message to Congress the slaveholding aristocracy were generally in a high state of excitement, because of the election of Mr. Lincoln as President. "The indignation with which the result of the Presidential election was received in the Southern States," says Jefferson Davis in his Short History of the Confederate States of America,[51] "proceeded from no personal hostility to the President-elect, nor from chagrin at the defeat of the Democratic candidates, but from the fact that the people of the South (the slaveholding aristocracy) recognized in Mr. Lincoln the representative of a party professing principles destructive to 'their peace, their prosperity, and their domestic tranquillity.'"

Again he says: "The character of the President in power now became an important factor in the situation. Mr. Buchanan's freedom from sectional asperity, his long life in the public service, his conciliatory disposition, his love of peace, and his reverence for the Constitution, were guarantees that he would not precipitate a conflict with any of the States. But it soon became evident that in the closing months of his administration he had little power to mould the policy of the future. Like all intelligent and impartial students of constitutional history, the President held that the Fed-

---

[51]Published in 1890, by Belford Co., New York. See p. 37.

eral Government had no rightful power to coerce
a State; and that although Congress may possess
many means of preserving it by conciliation, the
sword was not placed in their hand to preserve it
by force. Ten years before the date of this message, Mr. Calhoun had uttered similar sentiments
in the Senate."

Again, in the same work, Mr. Davis says:[52]
"Shortly after the election in November, the Senators and Representatives of Mississippi were invited by the Governor to meet him for consultation as to the character of the message he should
send to the special session of the Legislature he
had called to consider the propriety of assembling
a convention.[53]

"While holding, with my political associates,
that the right of a State to secede was unquestion-
able, the knowledge I had gained, as Chairman of
the Military Committee of the United States Senate and as Secretary of War, had made me familiar with the entire lack of preparation for war in
the South; and as, unlike most of my associates, I
did not believe that secession would be peaceably
accomplished, but that war would surely ensue between the sections, and that the odds against us
would be far greater than what were due merely
to our numerical inferiority, I was slower and more
reluctant than others, who held a different opinion,
to resort to that remedy. * * * While engaged in
consultation, I received a telegraphic message from

[52]See p. 40.
[53]Secession convention.

two members of President Buchanan's Cabinet, urging me to proceed immediately to Washington. Advised by my associates to comply, I hastened to the Capital and called on the President, who offered to read me his forthcoming message. I made certain suggestions for its modification, all of which he kindly accepted, but some of which he subsequently changed."

Thus, while this man and others were plotting against their country, he was sent for in haste and taken into the confidence of the President of the United States, and invited to make suggestions as to what his message to the Congress of the United States should contain. As to what suggestions were made the reader can draw his own conclusions in the light of the history of that time. If, instead of this, the President had treated Davis and his co-conspirators, as were Catiline and his co-conspirators against the life of the Roman Republic, in the days of Cicero, the rebellion would have been nipped in the bud and the President would have been crowned with glory. But instead of that he took him into his confidence and permitted his sympathies for the slave power to direct his course in another direction, and thereby went out of office in disgrace.

When the President's message was read in Congress, Senator Jefferson Davis publicly objected to portions of it; but not, of course, to that part wherein the President had said that neither he as the Executive of the Nation, nor any other department of the Government of the United States, had the power to coerce a State to remain in the Union. But these objections were puerile and only made for effect on the public mind; for what did Mr. Davis and his co-conspirators care for his doctrine that a State had no right to secede from the Union, so long as the President had announced as his conclusion that the Government had no power given it under the Constitution to coerce a State to remain in the Union; and that, owing to the condition of affairs in the South, he was unable to enforce the laws of the United States therein. This attitude of the President towards the rebellious States, greatly encouraged the conspirators and their Southern friends, to push secession as rapidly as possible, and to organize a new Government while Mr. Buchanan should remain in office.

The President was in sympathy with the South, and hence did not want to do anything to alienate his Southern friends. He pretended to believe that the South had suffered "serious grievances," and his idea seemed to be that those grievances ought to be redressed. In this condition of mind, from the time of the delivery of his message, he exerted all his influence in favor of compromise measures with the South, as he pretended the Union could not be preserved in any other way. He did not comprehend that the time for compromises with the slave-holding aristocracy was past; that the real question then was, Shall the Government of the United States permit them to run it in their own way or destroy the Republic?

In a special message to Congress on the 8th of January, 1861, the President, after. depicting the consequences which had already resulted to the Republic from the bare apprehension of civil war and the dissolution of the Union, said:

"Let the question be transferred from political assemblies to the ballot box, and the people themselves would speedily redress the serious grievances which the South have suffered. But, in Heaven's name, let the trial be made before we plung‧ into armed conflict upon the mere assumption that there is no other alternative. Time is a great conservative power. Let us pause at this momentous point and afford the people, both North and South, an opportunity for reflection. Would that South Carolina had been convinced of this truth before her precipitate action! I, therefore, appeal through you to the people of the country, to declare in their might that the Union must and shall be preserved by all constitutional means. I most earnestly recommend that you devote yourselves exclusively to the question how this can be accomplished in peace. All other questions, when compared with this, sink into insignificance. The present is no time for palliatives; action, prompt action, is required. A delay in Congress to prescribe or to recommend a distinct and practical proposition for conciliation, may drive us to a point from which it will be almost impossible to recede.

"A common ground on which conciliation and harmony can be produced is surely not unattainable. The proposition to compromise by letting the North have exclusive control of the territory above a certain line, and to give Southern institutions protection below that line, ought to receive universal approbation. In itself, indeed, it may not be entirely satisfactory, but when the alternative is between a reasonable concession on both sides and a dissolution of the Union, it is an imputation on the patriotism of Congress to assert that its members will hesitate for a moment."

This recommendation was totally disregarded, although compromise measures were introduced in Congress, but they rightfully failed. The friends of freedom and of the Union were not willing any longer to compromise with the slave power on their own terms; nor, indeed, on any terms other than to obey the laws of the land, and become loyal citizens of the Republic. On the other hand, the slaveholding aristocracy had made up their minds to spurn compromises and set up a Government of their own. All talk on their part in favor of compromise was only to gain time to carry out their plans of secession. For they had determined to destroy the Republic, rather than to see the power of the Nation pass into the hands of the friends of freedom.

CHAPTER IX.

CAUSES OF THE REBELLION.

When Mr. Lincoln was inaugurated President, on the 4th of March, 1861, rebellion was rampant. He found the Treasury empty, the army and navy scattered, forts and other property of the United States in possession of the rebels, and disloyalty in all the departments of the Government. He found the slave-holding aristocracy seeking to destroy the Government which they ceased to rule.

The leaders of that aristocracy made the election of Lincoln the pretext for attempting the destruction of the Union.

The real cause, however, lay deeper. The real cause was the great antagonism existing between a civilization based on free men, free speech, free schools, and free labor; and a civilization based on an aristocracy, bottomed on slavery, and opposed to these.

As slavery produced the latter civilization, so it was the primary cause of the rebellion. Slavery produced a condition which, in the course of events, made rebellion not only possible, but probable and desirable on the part of those who originated and promoted it; or, in other words, the ambition, avarice, and selfishness of man, made a condition which, in turn, produced rebellion. Indeed, without that condition, in all probability, the rebellion would not have occurred. But, in human affairs, man does not always do right. Selfish interests impel him to the wrong; and when the time comes

—as it always does—to right the wrong or the wrong seeks to trample down the right, a conflict ensues, which, in governmental affairs especially, sometimes ends in rebellion. For, says Madison, "Wherever there is an interest and power to do wrong, wrong will generally be done."

The Author of our being, however, does not compel any one to pursue this or that course; but He permits each to choose the course he desires to pursue. He points out, indeed, the way of right and how to avoid the wrong, but leaves to each the choosing as between the right and the wrong. When the wrong is chosen and pursued not only the wrong-doer, but others suffer from the consequences of his acts. As with individuals, so it is with states and nations.

There were but two causes for the rebellion— and only two. One primary, the other immediate. Many historians, however, give more. But the causes given do not agree with facts, and are neither logical nor philosophical; they mistake effects for causes.

I have already given the primary cause of the rebellion. Its immediate cause was the loss of power to promote a wrong condition; namely, a civilization based on slavery.

Long continued power is sweet, especially to those who arrogate to themselves the right to rule; and when power becomes thoroughly intrenched the history of the world shows that it is not given up without a struggle. The leaders of the slave-holding aristocracy, so long in power, determined not to give it up without a struggle. Beaten at the ballot box, they resorted to conspiracy and rebellion, and finally to the sword. If they could not rule the Union, in their way, they would break it and set up a Government of their own in accord with their civilization, over which their power would be supreme.

The declaration of a leading and distinguished Southern statesman—John C. Calhoun of South Carolina—made years before, was now being carried out.

"When we cease," he said, "thus to control this Nation through a disjointed democracy, or any material obstacle in that party which shall tend to throw us out of that rule and control, we shall then resort to the dissolution of the Union."

CHAPTER X.

THE NEW PRESIDENT INAUGURATED.

Mr. Lincoln entered upon his duties as President under great and trying difficulties. He was destined, however, to guide the ship of state through the storm of rebellion, now lashing itself into fury against the Government at Washington. Under this chaotic condition of things, when the Union seemed about to be going down into the darkness of oblivion, he was inaugurated President of the United States. The question now in every mind was, What will President Lincoln do to preserve the Union?

In his inaugural address, after speaking fully
as to the question of slavery and saying, "I have
no purpose, directly or indirectly, to interfere with
the institution of slavery in the States where it
exists. I believe I have no lawful right to do so,
and I have no inclination to do so," he further
said:

"I take the official oath to-day with no mental
reservations, and with no purpose to construe the
Constitution or laws by any hypercritical rules.
* * * It is seventy-two years since the first inauguration of a President under our National Constitution. During that period fifteen different and
very distinguished citizens have in succession administered the executive branch of the Government. They have conducted it through many per-
ils, and generally with great success. Yet, with
all this scope for precedent, I now enter upon the
same task, for the brief constitutional term of four
years, under great and peculiar difficulties.

"A disruption of the Federal Union, heretofore
only menaced, is now formidably attempted. I
hold that in the contemplation of universal law and
of the Constitution, the union of these States is
perpetual. Perpetuity is implied, if not expressed,
in the fundamental law of all national governments. It is safe to assert that no government
proper ever had a provision in its organic law for
its own termination. Continue to execute all the
express provisions of our National Constitution,
and the Union will endure forever, it being impos-

sible to destroy it except by some action not provided for in the instrument itself.

"Again, if the United States be not a Government proper, but an association of States in the
nature of a contract merely, can it, as a contract,
be peaceably unmade by less than all the parties
who made it? One party to a contract may violate
it—break it, so to speak—but does it not require
all to lawfully rescind it? Descending from these
general principles, we find the proposition that in
legal contemplation the Union is perpetual, confirmed by the history of the Union itself.

"The Union is much older than the Constitution. It was formed, in fact, by the Articles of Association in 1774. It was matured and continued
in the Declaration of Independence in 1776. It
was further matured, and the faith of all the then
thirteen States expressly plighted and engaged
that it should be perpetual, by the Articles of Confederation in 1781; and, finally, in 1787, one of the
declared objects for ordaining and establishing the
Constitution was to form a more perfect Union.
But if the destruction of the Union by one, or by
a part only of the States, be lawfully possible, the
Union is less than before, the Constitution having
lost the vital element of perpetuity.

"It follows from these views that no State, upon
its own mere motion, can lawfully get out of the
Union; that resolves and ordinances to that effect
are legally void; and that acts of violence within
any State or States against the authority of the

United States are insurrectionary or revolutionary, according to circumstances.

"I therefore consider that, in view of the Constitution and the laws, the Union is unbroken, and, to the extent of my ability, I shall take care, as the Constitution itself expressly enjoins upon me, that the laws of the Union shall be faithfully executed in all the States. Doing this, which I deem to be only a simple duty on my part, I shall perfectly perform it, so far as practicable, unless my rightful masters, the American people, shall withold the requisition, or in some authoritative manner direct the contrary. I trust this will not be regarded as a menace, but only as the declared purpose of the Union that it will constitutionally defend and maintain itself. In doing this, there need be no bloodshed or violence, and there shall be none unless it is forced upon the national authority. * * *

"That there are persons, in one section or another, who seek to destroy the Union at all events, and are glad of any pretext to do it, I will neither affirm nor deny. But if there be such, I need address no word to them.

"To those, however, who really love the Union, may I not speak, before entering upon so grave a matter as the destruction of our national fabric, with all its benefits, its memories, and its hopes? Would it not be well to ascertain why we do it? Will you hazard so desperate a step, while any portion of the ills you fly from have no real existence? Will you, while the certain ills you fly to are greater

than all the real ones you fly from? Will you risk
the commission of so fearful a mistake?

*   *   *   *   *   *

"If the minority will not acquiesce the majority
must, or the Government must cease. There is no
alternative for continuing the Government but ac-
quiescence on the one side or the other. If a minority in such a case will secede rather than acquiesce,
they make a precedent which in turn will ruin and
divide them, for a minority of their own will secede
from them whenever a majority refuses to be controlled by such a minority. For instance, why not
any portion of a new Confederacy, a year or two
hence, arbitrarily secede again, precisely as portions of the present Union now claim to secede
from it? All who cherish disunion sentiments are
now being educated to the exact temper of doing
this. Is there such perfect identity of interests
among the States to compose a new Union as to
produce harmony only, and prevent renewed secession? Plainly, the central idea of secession is the
essence of anarchy. * * * Physically speaking,
we cannot separate—we cannot remove our respective sections from each other, nor build an impas-
sable wall between them. * * * They cannot
but remain face to face; and intercourse, either
amicable or hostile, must continue between them.
Is it possible, then, to make that intercourse more
advantageous or more satisfactory after separation
than before? Can aliens make treaties easier than
friends can make laws? Can treaties be more faithfully enforced between aliens than laws can among

friends? Suppose you go to war, you cannot fight
always; and when, after much loss on both sides,
and no gain on either, you cease fighting, the iden-
tical questions as to terms of intercourse are again
upon you. * * *

"The Chief Magistrate derives all his authority from the people, and they have conferred none
upon him to fix the terms for the separation of the
States. The people themselves, also, can do this if
they choose, but the Executive, as such, has nothing to do with it. His duty is to administer the
present Government as it came to his hands, and
to transmit it unimpaired by him to his successor.
Why should there not be a patient confidence in
the ultimate justice of the people? * * * If the
Almighty Ruler of Nations, with his eternal truth
and justice, be on your side of the North, or on
yours of the South, that truth and that justice will
surely prevail by the judgment of this great tribu-
nal, the American people. * * * While the people
retain their virtue and vigilance, no administration, by any extreme wickedness or folly, can very
seriously injure the Government in the short space
of four years."

He closed his address by speaking directly to
those in rebellion against the Government, and
said:

"My countrymen, one and all, think calmly and
well upon this whole subject. Nothing valuable
can be lost by taking time. If there be an object
to hurry any of you, in hot haste, to a step
which you would never take deliberately, that ob-

ject will be frustrated by taking time; but no good object can be frustrated by it. Such of you as are now dissatisfied still have the old Constitution un-impaired, and on the sensitive point, the laws of your own framing under it; while the new adminis-tration will have no immediate power, if it would, to change either. If it were admitted that you who are dissatisfied hold the right side in the dispute, there is still no single reason for precipitate action. Intelligence, patriotism, Christianity, and a firm reliance on Him who has never yet forsaken this favored land, are still competent to adjust, in the best way, all our present difficulties.

"In your hands, my dissatisfied fellow country-men, and not in mine, is the momentous issue of civil war. The Government will not assail you. You can have no conflict without being yourselves the aggressors. You have no oath registered in heaven to destroy the Government, while I shall have the most solemn one to 'preserve, protect and defend it.'

"I am loath to close. We are not enemies, but friends. We must not be enemies. Though passion may have strained, it must not break our bonds of affection. The mystic chords of memory, stretch-ing from every battle field and patriot grave to every living heart and hearthstone, all over this broad land, will yet swell the chorus of the Union, when again touched, as surely they will be, by the better angels of our nature."[54]

---

[54] For address in full, see Harper's "Pictorial History of the Great Rebellion," p. 47.

CHAPTER XI.

THE BLACK CLOUD OF REBELLION.

This address made a profound impression on the people, and its influence was such that it seemed as though the black cloud of rebellion might pass away. But Lincoln's noble words were not heeded. The leaders of the South were impervious to reason. They were in bondage to a wrong condition—a bondage worse than chattel slavery. In fact, slavery injured the slaveholder more than the slave, for he who deprives another of his liberty violates law, and law always punishes its violation. I do not speak of human law, but of the "higher law." That law scourges the master and lets the slave go free. The law of nature says all men are born free; and, therefore, no one can be made a slave except by coercion—not by right. The Creator did not give man dominion over man; only over such things as the fishes of the sea, the fowls of the air, and the beasts of the field.

The leaders of the South by reason of being in bondage to that wrong condition were in such a state of mind that they were willing to wage war against the Government, although by so doing they might render themselves liable to the penalty not only of human law, but to that of the higher law, which says, "Woe unto the world because of offences, for it must needs be that offences come; but woe to that man by whom the offence cometh."

In consequence of the President's words it re-

quired the efforts of their most fiery orators to re-
kindle the flame of secession.

Virginia, old Virginia—the birthplace, home,
and final resting place of the immortal Washington—hesitating to leave the Union and join the
Confederacy, one of the leaders of the rebellion—
Roger A. Pryor of Virginia—delivered a speech
on the 10th day of April at Charleston, South Carolina,[55] in response to a serenade, saying: "Gentlemen, I thank you, especially that you have at last
annihilated this accursed Union, reeking with corruption and insolent with excess of tyranny.
Thank God, it is at last blasted and riven by the
lightning wrath of an outraged and indignant people. Not only is it gone, but gone forever. * * *
For my part, gentlemen, if Abraham Lincoln and
Hannibal Hamlin to-morrow were to abdicate their
offices and were to give me a blank sheet of paper
to write the conditions of reannexation to the de-
funct Union, I would scornfully spurn the over-
ture. * * *

"I invoke you, in your demonstrations of popular opinion, in your exhibitions of official intent,
to give no countenance to this idea of reconstruc-
tion. * * * I pray you, gentlemen, rob them
of that idea. Proclaim to the world that upon no
condition, and under no circumstance, will South
Carolina ever again enter into political association with the Abolitionists of New England.

"Do not distrust Virginia. As sure as to-mor-

_____

[55]A secession convention was then in session in Virginia, in
which the Unionists were holding the secessionists in check.

row's sun will rise upon us, just so sure will Virginia be a member of this Southern Confederation. And I will tell you, gentlemen, what will put her in the Southern Confederation in less than an hour by Shrewsbury clock—strike a blow! The very moment that blood is shed, old Virginia will make common cause with her sisters of the South. It is impossible she should do otherwise."

On the next day, April 11, the President of the Southern Confederacy, some of his Cabinet, and other gentlemen, were discussing in the office of General Walker, Secretary of War, the advisability of immediately opening fire on Fort Sumter. The Secretary of War seemed to be opposed to the proposition, when a prominent gentleman of Alabama, who was present, said: "Sir, unless you sprinkle blood in the face of the people of Alabama they will be back in the old Union in less than ten days!"

Robert Toombs of Georgia, Secretary of State, said to Mr. Davis that he thought it unwise to attack Fort Sumter. "The firing upon that fort," said he, "will inaugurate a civil war greater than any the world has yet seen. * * * You will wantonly strike a hornet's nest, which extends from mountains to ocean, and legions now quiet will swarm out and sting us to death. It is unnecessary; it puts us in the wrong; it is fatal."[56]

The order was given, however, and, in this state of mind, the leaders crossed the Rubicon of rebellion, and struck the blow.

[56]Stovall's "Life of Toombs," p. 226.

Old Virginia now went out of the Union, joined the Confederacy, became the great battle field of the South, and reaped the bitter fruit of rebellion.

CHAPTER XII.

FORT SUMTER.

Early in the morning of April 12, 1861, Treason fired its first shot on Fort Sumter.[57] That shot was the challenge to the final conflict between the two civilizations. The world never beheld a more momentous issue—one in which so much to humanity was at stake. It was the beginning of a war between civilizations—a war between right and wrong.

When Freedom accepted that challenge, Treason attempted to justify its conduct to the world through Jefferson Davis, President of the Southern Confederacy. In an elaborate message to the Confederate Congress, at Montgomery, Alabama, on April 29, he set forth to the world their reasons for the steps which had been taken.

"The declaration of war," he said, "made against this Confederacy by Abraham Lincoln, President of the United States, in his proclamation, issued on the 15th day of the present month,[58] ren-

---

[57] A fort belonging to the United States in Charleston harbor, South Carolina.

[58] This proclamation was issued by President Lincoln April 15th, 1861, after the firing on Fort Sumter by the rebels. In that proclamation the President called for 75,000 volunteer soldiers for the purpose of aiding to suppress unlawful "combinations" of persons, in the States in rebellion against the government of the United

ders it necessary, in my judgment, that you should
convene at the earliest practicable moment to devise the measures necessary for the defense of the
country. The occasion is, indeed, an extraordinary
one. It justifies me in giving a brief review of the
relations heretofore existing between us and the
States which now unite in warfare against us, and
a succinct statement of the events which have
resulted, to the end that mankind may pass intelligent and impartial judgment on our motives
and objects."

After reviewing the slavery question from the
beginning of the Government of the United States,
the right of a State to secede, and other matters,
he said, in justification of their acts:

"Finally, a great party was organized for the
purpose of obtaining the administration of the
Government, with the avowed object of using its
power for the total exclusion of the slave States
from all participation in the benefits of the public
domain acquired by all the States in common,
whether by conquest or purchase, surrounding
them entirely by States in which slavery should be
prohibited, thus rendering the property in slaves
so insecure as to be comparatively worthless, and
thereby annihilating in effect property worth thou-

States, "and to cause the laws to be duly executed." And he commanded the persons composing said combinations "to disperse and
retire peaceably to their respective abodes within twenty days from
this date." The President also ordered an extra session of Congress to convene on the 4th day of July, "to consider and determine
such measures, as in their wisdom, the public safety and interest
may seem to demand." The President appealed "to all loyal citizens
to favor, facilitate, and aid this effort to maintain the honor, the
integrity, and existence of our national Union, and the perpetuity
of popular government, and to redress wrongs already long enough
endured."

sands of millions of dollars. This party, thus organized, succeeded in the month of November last in the election of its candidate for the Presidency of the United States.

"In the meantime, under the mild and genial climate of the Southern States, and the increasing care for the well-being and comfort of the laboring classes, dictated alike by interest and humanity, the African slaves had augmented in number from about six hundred thousand, at the date of the adoption of the constitutional compact, to upward of four millions. In a moral and social condition they had been elevated from brutal savages into docile, intelligent, and civilized agricultural laborers, and supplied not only with bodily comforts, but with careful religious instruction, under the supervision of a superior race. Their labor had been so directed as not only to allow a gradual and marked amelioration of their own condition, but to convert hundreds of thousands of square miles of the wilderness into cultivated lands covered with a prosperous people. Towns and cities had sprung into existence, and it rapidly increased in wealth and population under the social system of the South. The white population of the Southern slave-holding States had augmented from about 1,250,000 at the date of the adoption of the Constitution to more than 8,500,000 in 1860, and the productions of the South in cotton, rice, sugar, and tobacco, for the full development and continuance of which the labor of African slaves was and is indispensable, had swollen to an amount which formed nearly three-fourths of the export of the whole United States, and had become absolutely necessary to the wants of civilized man.

"With interests of such overwhelming magnitude imperiled, the people of the Southern States were driven by the conduct of the North to the adoption of some course of action to avoid the dangers with which they were openly menaced. * * *

"We feel that our cause is just and holy. We protest solemnly, in the face of mankind, that we desire peace at any sacrifice save that of honor. * * * All we ask is to be let alone—that those who never held power over us shall not now attempt our subjugation by arms. This we will, we must resist, to the direst extremity. The moment this pretension is abandoned, the sword will drop from our grasp, and we shall be ready to enter into treaties of amity and commerce that cannot but be mutually beneficial. So long as this pretension is maintained, with a firm reliance on that Divine Power which covers with its protection the just cause, we will continue to struggle for our own inherent right to freedom, independence, and self-government."[59]

[59] For the message in full, see Harper's "Pictorial History of the Great Rebellion," p. 113.

CHAPTER XIII.

A WICKED REBELLION.

In the previous chapter I have set forth the justification of the chief of the rebellion. What a
cold-blooded and selfish justification for rebelling
and making war against his country! Indeed,
such a justification could have emanated only from
one who had been long saturated with the virus
of slavery.

Mr. Davis rightly said, "The occasion is, indeed,
an extraordinary one." For it would appear, from
his message, that because "a great party was organized for the purpose of obtaining the administration of the Government, with the avowed object
of using its power for the total exclusion of the
slave States from all participation in the benefits
of the public domain;" and because "this party,
thus organized, succeeded in the month of November last in the election of its candidate for the
presidency of the United States," therefore, the
South was justified in its attempt to destroy the
Republic.

Is that a justification, even if all the statements
of Mr. Davis were true? But it is not true that the
new party, he speaks of, denied the slave States
the right of "all participation in the benefits of the
public domain," but only the right of extending
slavery. Its doctrine was, that slavery must be
confined to the States where it already existed.
In other words, it believed that freedom should be

national, slavery local—confined to where it already existed.

For a complete answer to the attempted justification of Mr. Davis in his message, the reader is referred to the words of Mr. Stephens, in his speech against secession.[60] In that speech he seems to have anticipated some such justification as that made by Davis. In his closing paragraph he said: "Now, for you, to attempt to overthrow such a Government as this, under which we have lived for more than three-quarters of a century—in which we have gained our wealth, our standing as a Nation, our domestic safety while the elements of peril are around us, with peace and tranquillity, accompanied with unbounded prosperity and rights unassailed—is the height of madness, folly, and wickedness."

Mr. Davis, in his "Short History of the Confederate States of America,"[61] says: "The common opinion in the Southern States was that the separation would be final but peaceful. For my own part, while believing that secession was a right and properly a peaceful remedy, I had never believed that it would be permitted to be peacefully exercised. I had predicted a long and desperate struggle, and advised preparations to be made therefor. Very few in the South agreed with me

[60]For speech see p. 100, ante.
[61]See page 59. Mr. Davis in that work says on page 84, "It is not my purpose in this volume to describe the battles of the war. * * * My sole object is to vindicate the rightful action of the Southern people in maintaining the sovereignty of their States against wrongful and unconstitutional usurpation of power by their common agent, the Federal Government, and to defend them from the aspersions of unscrupulous partisans who have maligned as rebels and traitors men true to their allegiance and defenders of the Constitution."

at that time, and my opinions were as unwelcome as they were unexpected."

Thus, to promote a great wrong, this man, and others—especially this man—believing that secession would cause "a long and desperate struggle," counseled that it be done; and "advised preparations to be made" for that coming struggle.

To obtain power they were willing to make war on the Government, and to sacrifice hundreds of thousands of lives and billions of treasure.

In order to show in what light the slave-holding aristocracy of the South viewed the people of the North and the cause, the real cause of the war, I give the statement of one of the leading editors of the South, published in 1862.[62]

"This has been called," he said, "a fratricidal war by some; by others an irrepressible conflict between freedom and slavery. We respectfully take issue with the authors of both these ideas. We are not the brothers of the Yankees, and the slavery question is merely the pretext, not the cause of the war. The true irrepressible conflict lies fundamentally in the hereditary hostility, the sacred animosity, the eternal antagonism between the two races engaged.

"The Norman Cavalier cannot brook the vulgar familiarity of the Saxon Yankee, while the latter is continually devising some plan to bring down his aristocratic neighbor to his own detested level. Thus was the contest waged in the old United States. So long as Dickinson doughfaces were to

[62]Harper's "Pictorial History of the Great Rebellion," p. 17.

be bought, and Cochrane cowards to be frightened, so long was the Union tolerable to Southern men; but when, owing to division in our own ranks, the Yankee hirelings placed one of their own spawn (Lincoln) over us, political connection became unendurable and separation necessary to preserve our self-respect.

"As our Norman kinsman in England, always a minority, have ruled their Saxon countrymen in political vassalage up to the present day, so have we, the 'slave oligarchs,' governed the Yankees till within a twelve-month. We framed the Constitution, for seventy years moulded the policy of the Government, and placed our own men, or 'Northern men with Southern principles,' in power. On the 6th of November, 1860, the Puritans emancipated themselves, and are now in violent insurrection against their former owners. This insane holiday freak will not last long, however, for, dastards in fight, and incapable of self-government, they will inevitably again fall under the control of the superior race."

History bears out this statement as being the feeling of the aristocracy of the South towards the people of the North. They differed, however, among themselves as to the cause of their rebelling.

No wonder Jefferson exclaimed in the beginning of the Nation, in regard to slavery: "I tremble for my country when I reflect that God is just; that His justice cannot sleep forever. * * * The Almighty has no attribute which can take side with us in such a contest." Or that he uttered those other prophetic words: "We must wait with patience the workings of an overruling Providence, and hope that that is preparing the deliverance of these our brethren. When the measure of their tears shall be full, when their groans shall have involved heaven itself in darkness, doubtless a God of Justice will awaken to their distress. Nothing is more certainly written in the Book of Fate than that this people shall be free."

Can there be found in all history a rebellion more wicked than this one? When the claimed cause, given by those in rebellion, is examined is it not found absolutely unjustifiable, instead of "just and holy," as characterized by Mr. Davis?

In the language of another historian: "The awful responsibility for shedding of blood, for carnage, cruelty, suffering, distress, and the thousand evils attendant upon war, must rest upon the men who, without any just or reasonable cause, began the rebellion of 1861, and persevered in it four weary, desolating years." What a fearful responsibility! But such is the verdict of unbiased history.

There is an attempt being made, however, in these days to pervert the truth of history and gloss over the acts of these men and the cause they represented—to make them respectable instead of odious. But it should never be forgotten that there were but two great parties in those days—"patriots and traitors," as classified by Senator Stephen A.

Douglas.[63] One for the Union, the other against;
one for the rights of man, the other against; one
for the principle that all men are created equal,
the other against; one for free men, the other
against; one for free speech, the other against; one
for free schools, the other against; one for free
labor, the other against; one for the dignity of
labor, the other for its degradation; one for liberty,
the other against; one for country, the other
against; one for the Republic established by the
fathers, the other against; one for a civilization
based on Freedom, the other for a civilization based
on Slavery.

It is the bounden duty of the historian to turn
on the light, however unpleasant it may be to do
so, that the truth may be seen; so that the generations yet to come may be enabled to "pass intelligent and impartial judgment" on the "motives and
objects" of those who originated and were engaged
in promoting that rebellion. Shall we distort history in order to smooth the pathway of those who
have been engaged on the side of wrong? Is that
the province of the historian? Rather should not
the truth be told, as in the Scriptures, so that posterity may guard against a repetition of the wrong?
Wrong may be forgiven, but history is inexorable.

[63]In his great speech at Chicago, in 1861, after the firing on Fort
Sumter.

CHAPTER XIV.

THE CLOSING DRAMA.

When Abraham Lincoln uttered the words,[64] "That is the real issue. It is the eternal struggle between these two principles—right and wrong—throughout the world," little did he think that in so short a time he would be at the head of the Nation, and that a gigantic rebellion would be going on to maintain the "wrong" of that issue, and to destroy that Nation and erect another with slavery as its chief corner-stone. But so it was. The supreme test of republican institutions was at hand. War, grim war—civil war—was upon the Nation. Who could tell the result? If the Republic went down there would be no hope for liberty and self-government for ages.

Would the eloquent and prophetic words of Webster now be verified? A few months before his death, in 1852, he said: "The world will cry out 'Shame' upon us, if we show ourselves unworthy to be the descendants of those great and illustrious men, who fought for their liberty, and secured it to their posterity, by the Constitution of the United States. * * *

"On Washington's principles, and under the guidance of his example, will we and our children uphold the Constitution. Under his military leadership our fathers conquered; and under the outspread banner of his political and constitutional principles will we also conquer. To that

[64] In his debate with Douglas, in 1858.

standard we shall adhere, and uphold it through evil and through good report. We will meet danger, we will meet death, if they come, in its protection; and we will struggle on, in daylight and in darkness; ay, in the thickest darkness, with all the storms which it may bring with it, till 'Danger's troubled night is o'er, and the star of Peace return.'"

The world did not have an opportunity to cry out "Shame," for the President and the loyal people of the Nation, rose to the occasion. More than two million men were mustered against the hosts of Treason. For four long years the battle raged with fury.

What a grand army was that! the volunteer army of the United States. It was composed of men and beardless youths from all avocations of life. The farmer left his plow; the blacksmith dropped his hammer; the carpenter forsook his bench; the lawyer laid aside his brief, and the doctor quit his patient; the preacher left the sacred desk; young men went from the desk and counter, from the office, field and factory, from the shop, and all from the fireside of loved ones. "Good-bye" was said to friends most dear, and they went forth to do, and, if need be, die for their country.

Battle after battle was fought, and the battlefields were strewn with the slain and wounded; hospitals were filled with the wounded and suffering; prison pens were filled with the captured, and many were tortured and starved to death. Hundreds of thousands went down to death that the

Nation might live. They sacrificed home and its sweet memories, loved ones, and life, while in the full vigor of manhood.

That was an army of intelligence, patriotism and courage. Of this there can be no question. General Grant,[65] its great chieftain, the heroic man of the age, said of it in his report of the siege of Vicksburg: "It is a striking feature, so far as my observation goes, of the present volunteer army of the United States, that there is nothing which men are called upon to do, mechanical or professional, that accomplished adepts cannot be found for the duty required in almost every regiment." And, again, he said, in his farewell address to the army, that its "marches, sieges, and battles, in distance, duration, resolution, and brilliancy of results, dims the luster of the world's past military achievements, and will be the patriot's precedent in defense of liberty and right, in all time to come."

Its patriotism and courage were fully attested by the more than two thousand battles and skirmishes which it fought, with a vigilant and courageous foe on its own soil; by the long marches and untold privations it endured, by day and by night, in a climate to which it was not inured; and, final-

---

[65]General U. S. Grant was born at Point Pleasant, Ohio, April 27, 1822. Graduated at United States Military Academy, 1843. Served in the Mexican War, and was promoted to captain, 1853. Resigned commission, 1854, and afterward engaged in the tanning business at Galena, Ill. Entered the Civil War as colonel Twenty-first Illinois Volunteers. Promoted to brigadier general, July, 1861, then to major general; then to lieutenant general, March, 1864. Received surrender of Gen. Robt. E. Lee of the Confederate army, at Appomattox, April 9, 1865. Commissioned general, a grade created for him, by Congress, July 25, 1866. Elected President of the United States, 1868, 1872. Died, July 23, 1885. General Grant's services to the Republic were of inestimable value; and he will go down in history as one of the greatest military chieftains of the world.

ly, by the great victory it achieved for the right, and then quietly dispersed to their homes and again entered upon the peaceful pursuits of good citizens of a saved Republic, without having imposed conditions upon its enemy other than that of becoming loyal citizens of the Union.

One reason for its strong patriotism and courage is that it did not fight for conquest—as a Caesar or an Alexander—but for liberty, and country. It fought to maintain that civilization which it is hoped will become the civilization of the world.

By the heroic efforts of that army that civilization, whose germ was planted in Virginia, surrendered at Appomattox to that civilization whose germ was planted on the rocky shores of Massachusetts, and a new civilization was born with freedom to all as its chief corner-stone. Then, universal freedom was made the supreme law of the land.

While millions were rejoicing over the great victory of "right" over "wrong," and while peace—blessed peace!—was dawning upon a stricken land, the President—our beloved Lincoln—was struck down by an assassin, and joy was turned into mourning. "With malice towards none, with charity for all," his great soul took its departure; and Liberty, in all lands, mourned his death.

"Chieftain, farewell! The Nation mourns thee. Mothers shall teach thy name to their lisping children. The youth of our land shall emulate thy virtues. Statesmen shall study thy record and learn lessons of wisdom. Mute though thy lips be, yet they still speak. Hushed is thy voice, but its echoes of liberty are ringing through the world, and the sons of bondage listen with joy. Prisoned thou art in death, and yet thou art marching abroad, and chains and manacles are bursting at thy touch. Thou didst fall not for thyself. The assassin had no hate for thee. Our hearts were aimed at, our national life was sought. We crown thee as our martyr, and humanity enthrones thee as her triumphant son. Hero, martyr, friend, fare-well!"[66]

The corner-stone of National Independence has now long been in its place; and on it is inscribed the name of George Washington.

The Union soldier placed another stone by its side—the Declaration of Independence, with all its promises fulfilled. On this stone Liberty inscribes the name of Abraham Lincoln.

------

[66]Closing paragraph of Bishop Simpson's oration, delivered at the funeral of President Lincoln, Oak Ridge Cemetery, near Springfield, Ill., May 4, 1865.

BOOK II.

Landmarks of the Formative Period of the Republic.

BOOK II.

CHAPTER I.

What may be called the actual formative period of the Republic, and the Union of the United States of America, extended over a period of about fifteen years, beginning with the first Continental Congress, in September, 1774, and ending with the adoption of the Constitution by the people in 1787-88.

During that time the Government of the Union passed thrugh three stages or forms: 1. The Revolutionary. 2. The Confederate. 3. The Constitutional. But while the Revolutionary and Confederate periods have passed away, the Constitutional still exists; and will continue to exist until the people shall see fit to change the Constitution, and the government under it, to some other form.

While the Revolutionary War was going on, and soon after the Declaration of Independence was promulgated, the Articles of Confederation were formed by the Continental Congress, and sent to the several States for their ratification; but they were not ratified by all until March 1, 1781, Maryland being the last State to approve them. These articles were not to be binding on any of the States until they should receive the approval of all.

On the second day of March, 1781, Congress

assembled under the Confederation; and the Government was carried on under these articles until the Constitution—which was the next step in the formation of the Republic—was adopted and went into effect.

By an act of Congress the Government was to begin operations under the Constitution on the 4th day of March, 1789. Congress assembled on that day, but Washington, the first President, was not inaugurated until the 30th day of April. Since the Constitution went into effect it has been the fundamental and supreme law of the land—although assailed by internal foes—together with the amendments, which have, from time to time, been adopted and become a part of it.

These instruments, together with the Ordinance of 1787, which was adopted by the Congress in July, 1787, a short time prior to the formation and adoption of the Constitution by the convention, which met at Philadelphia, are herein set forth, with sketches of the origin of each, for the convenience and benefit of those who may study the formation of our Republic. I have also appended an Index and Analysis of the Constitution, as an aid to its study.

The following suggestions are made to students of the Constitution: First, read the Constitution carefully. Next, study the Index and Analysis thoroughly. And lastly, go over both again and again, and again, until its contents are as familiar as the Ten Commandments.

CHAPTER II.

THE DECLARATION OF INDEPENDENCE.

SKETCH OF THE ORIGIN OF THE DECLARATION—TEXT OF
THE DECLARATION.

The first Continental or General Congress of
the Colonies met in Carpenter's Hall, Philadelphia,
September 5, 1774. In it were forty-four delegates, representing eleven of the thirteen colonies.
Later, eleven more delegates took their seats, and
all of the colonies were then represented except
Georgia, which promised to concur with "her sister colonies" in their effort to maintain their rights
as English subjects. Peyton Randolph, of Virginia, was elected President of the Congress.
Many distinguished men were delegates. Among
the number were Washington, Richard Henry Lee,
Patrick Henry, John Adams, Samuel Adams, John
Dickinson, William Livingston, John Jay, Roger
Sherman, and the Rutledges of South Carolina.

On the 14th of October the Congress adopted a
Declaration of Colonial Rights, and on the 26th a
Petition to the King,[1] asking the redress of their
wrongs, was also adopted.

The second Continental Congress met in Philadelphia, in the State House (Independence Hall),
May 10, 1775, a few days after the battles of Lexington and Concord. This time Georgia was represented along with all the rest of the colonies. A
second Petition to the King was formulated and

[1] George III.

adopted, and Washington was appointed commander-in-chief of the Continental army, though
Congress still denied any intention of separating
from Great Britain and earnestly expressed a desire for the peaceful settlement of all difficulties.[2]

But the king, instead of taking notice of these
petitions, and righting the wrongs of the
colonists, declared the colonies in rebellion and
sent more troops over to force them to submit to
the many unjust and tyrannical measures imposed
upon them. The colonists now began to realize
that they must back down and become slaves to a
tyrant or fight for their rights as free men. They
at once determined on the latter course.

Patrick Henry said: "We must fight! An appeal to arms and to the God of Hosts is all that is
left us. I repeat it, sir, we must fight!" Washington declared that, "nothing short of Independence,
it appears to me, can possibly do." The Sons of
Liberty echoed this sentiment until the Congress
finally became possessed with the idea that "nothing short of Independence" would do. The idea
of a separation from the mother country began to
dawn upon them as the only thing they could do
to promote their welfare and happiness as a
people.

This idea took shape in 1776. On the 7th of
June of that year Richard Henry Lee, of Virginia,

[2]It was of this Congress, and of these their doings, that Lord
Chatham said: "'For genuine sagacity, for singular moderation, for
solid wisdom, manly spirit, sublime sentiments, and simplicity of
language, for everything respectable and honorable, the Congress
of Philadelphia shine unrivalled. This wise people speak out. They
do not hold the language of slaves; they tell you what they mean.
They do not ask you to repeal your laws as a favor; they claim it
as a right."

arose in his place in the Congress and moved, "That these United Colonies are, and, of right, ought to be, free and independent States; and that all political connection between them and the State of Great Britain is, and ought to be, totally suppressed."[3] John Adams, of Massachusetts, seconded the motion. Upon this resolution there sprang up at once, after it had been referred to a committee of the whole, an earnest and powerful debate. It was opposed by some, principally on the ground that it was prematures. If passed they felt that reconciliation would be no longer possible. It meant that the colonies must establish their full and final sovereignty or be conquered and enslaved; that thenceforward there could be no retreat.

The resolution was debated until the 10th, when it was adopted in committee. On the same day a committee, consisting of Thomas Jefferson, John Adams, Benjamin Franklin, Roger Sherman, and Robert R. Livingston, was appointed and instructed to prepare a formal declaration "that these United Colonies are, and of right ought to be, free and independent States; that they are absolved from all allegiance to the British crown; and that all political connection between them and the State of Great Britain is, and ought to be, dissolved." At the same time Lee's resolution was postponed until the 1st of July, to give time for

[3]On the 10th of May, Congress had, by resolution, recommended the establishment of independent State governments in all the colonies. This, however, was not sufficiently national to suit the bolder and wiser members of that body, and many of the people at large. Lee's resolution more fully expressed the popular will.

working up the idea of a total separation from
the mother country. The postponement was immediately followed by proceedings in the colonies,
in most of which the delegates in Congress were
either instructed or authorized to vote for Independence.

On the 28th of June the committee made their
report and presented the Declaration which they
had drawn up. The first or original draft
was prepared by Thomas Jefferson, chairman of
the committee, and but few alterations were made
in it by the committee or by Congress. On the 2d
of July Congress proceeded to the consideration
of this great paper. The discussion of it lasted
for nearly three days. It was so powerfully opposed by some that Jefferson compared the opposition to "the ceaseless action of gravity, weigh-
ing upon us by night and by day." Its supporters,
however, were the leading minds and urged its
adoption with an ability and an eloquence only
born of a desire and a determination to be free
men. John Adams, Jefferson says, was "the Co-
lossus in that debate," and "fought fearlessly for
every word of it."

Finally, on the 4th day of July, 1776, the paper,
known as the Declaration of Independence, was
agreed to, and the transaction is recorded as follows in the journal for that day:

Agreeably to the order of the day, the Congress resolved itself into a committee of the whole,
to take into their further consideration the Declaration; and, after some time, the President re-

sumed the chair, and Mr. Harrison reported that
the committee have agreed to a declaration, which
they desired him to report. The Declaration being
read, was agreed to as follows:

A DECLARATION BY THE REPRESENTATIVES OF THE
UNITED STATES OF AMERICA, IN CONGRESS
ASSEMBLED.

When, in the course of human events, it becomes necessary for one people to dissolve the
political bands which have connected them with
another, and to assume, among the powers of the
earth, the separate and equal station to which the
laws of nature and of nature's God entitle them,
a decent respect to the opinions of mankind requires that they should declare the causes which
impel them to the separation.

We hold these truths to be self-evident—that
all men are created equal; that they are endowed
by their Creator with certain inalienable rights;
that among these are life, liberty, and the pursuit
of happiness. That, to secure these rights, governments are instituted among men, deriving their
just powers from the consent of the governed; that,
whenever any form of government becomes destructive of these ends, it is the right of the people
to alter or abolish it, and to institute a new government, laying its foundations on such principles, and organizing its powers in such form, as
to them shall seem most likely to effect their safety
and happiness. Prudence, indeed, will dictate
that governments long established should not be
changed for light and transient causes; and, accordingly, all experience hath shown that man-

kind are more disposed to suffer, while evils are
sufferable, than to right themselves by abolishing
the forms to which they are accustomed. But
when a long train of abuses and usurpations, pur-
suing invariably the same object, evinces a design
to reduce them under absolute despotism, it is
their right, it is their duty, to throw off such government, and to provide new guards for their future security. Such has been the patient suffer-
ance of these colonies, and such is now the necessity which constrains them to alter their former
systems of government. The history of the present
King of Great Britain is a history of repeated
injuries and usurpations, all having in direct object the establishment of an absolute tyranny over
these States. To prove this, let facts be submitted to a candid world.

1.   He has refused his assent to laws the most
wholesome and necessary for the public good.

2.   He has forbidden his governors to pass
laws of immediate and pressing importance, unless
suspended in their operations till his assent should
be obtained; and, when so suspended, he has utterly neglected to attend to them.

3.   He has refused to pass other laws for the
accommodation of large districts of people, unless
those people would relinquish the right of representation in the Legislature—a right inestimable
to them, and formidable to tyrants only.

4.   He has called together legislative bodies at
places unusual, uncomfortable, and distant from
the repository of their public records, for the sole

purpose of fatiguing them into compliance with his measures.

5. He has dissolved representative houses repeatedly, for opposing, with manly firmness, his invasions on the rights of the people.

6. He has refused, for a long time after such dissolutions, to cause others to be elected, whereby the legislative powers, incapable of annihilation, have returned to the people at large for their exercise; the State remaining, in the meantime, exposed to all the dangers of invasions from without, and convulsions within.

7. He has endeavored to prevent the population of these States; for that purpose obstructing the laws for the naturalization of foreigners; refusing to pass others to encourage their migration hither, and raising the conditions of new appropriations of lands.

8. He has obstructed the administration of justice, by refusing his assent to laws for establishing judiciary powers.

9. He has made judges dependent on his will alone for the tenure of their offices, and the amount and payment of their salaries.

10. He has erected a multitude of new offices, and sent hither swarms of officers to harass our people and eat out their substance.

11. He has kept among us in times of peace, standing armies, without the consent of our Legislatures.

12. He has affected to render the military independent of, and superior to, the civil power.

13. He has combined with others to subject us to a jurisdiction foreign to our Constitutions, and unacknowledged by our laws; giving his assent to their acts of pretended legislation.

14. For quartering large bodies of armed troops among us.

15. For protecting them, by a mock trial, from punishment for any murders which they should commit on the inhabitants of these States.

16. For cutting off our trade with all parts of the world.

17. For imposing taxes on us without our consent.

18. For depriving us, in many cases, of the benefits of a trial by jury.

19. For transporting us beyond seas, to be tried for pretended offenses.

20. For abolishing the free system of English laws in a neighboring province, establishing therein an arbitrary government, and enlarging its boundaries, so as to render it at once an example and fit instrument for introducing the same absolute rule into these colonies.

21. For taking away our charters, abolishing our most valuable laws, and altering, fundamentally, the forms of our governments.

22. For suspending our own Legislatures, and declaring themselves invested with power to legislate for us in all cases whatsoever.

23. He has abdicated government here, by declaring us out of his protection, and waging war against us.

24. He has plundered our seas, ravaged our coasts, burned our towns, and destroyed the lives of our people.

25. He is at this time transporting large armies of foreign mercenaries to complete the works of death, desolation and tyranny, already begun with circumstances of cruelty and perfidy scarcely paralleled in the most barbarous ages, and totally unworthy the head of a civilized nation.

26. He has constrained our fellow citizens, taken captive on the high seas, to bear arms against their country, to become the executioners of their friends and brethren, or to fall themselves by their hands.

27. He has excited domestic insurrection among us, and has endeavored to bring on the inhabitants of our frontiers the merciless Indian savages, whose known rule of warfare is an undistinguished destruction of all ages, sexes, and conditions.

In every stage of these oppressions we have petitioned for redress in the most humble terms; our repeated petitions have been answered only by repeated injury. A prince whose character is thus marked by every act which may define a tyrant, is unfit to be the ruler of a free people.

Nor have we been wanting in our attentions to our British brethren. We have warned them, from time to time, of attempts by their Legislature to extend an unwarrantable jurisdiction over us. We have reminded them of the circum-

stances of our emigration and settlement here.
We have appealed to their native justice and magnanimity, and we have conjured them by the ties
of our common kindred to disavow these usurpations, which would inevitably interrupt our con-
nections and correspondence. They, too, have been
deaf to the voice of justice and of consanguinity.
We must, therefore, acquiesce in the necessity
which denounces our separation, and hold them
as we hold the rest of mankind—enemies in war;
in peace, friends.

We, therefore, the representatives of the United States of America in General Congress assembled, appealing to the Supreme Judge of the world
for the rectitude of our intentions, do, in the name
and by the authority of the good people of these
colonies, solemnly publish and declare that these
United Colonies are, and of right ought to be,
free and independent States; that they are absolved from all allegiance to the British crown,
and that all political connection between them
and the State of Great Britain is, and ought to be,
totally dissolved, and that, as free and independent States, they have full power to levy war, conclude peace, contract alliances, establish commerce, and do all other acts and things which independent States may of right do. And for the
support of this Declaration, with a firm reliance
on the protection of Divine Providence, we mutually pledge to each other our lives, our fortunes,
and our sacred honor.

The foregoing Declaration was, by order of

Congress, engrossed, and signed by the following members:

JOHN HANCOCK.

NEW HAMPSHIRE.
JOSIAH BARTLETT.
WILLIAM WHIPPLE. .
MATTHEW THORNTON.

RHODE ISLAND.
STEPHEN HOPKINS.
WILLIAM ELLERY.

NEW YORK.
WILLIAM FLOYD.
PHILIP LIVINGSTON.
FRANCIS LEWIS.
LEWIS MORRIS.

MASSACHUSETTS BAY.
SAMUEL ADAMS.
JOHN ADAMS.
ROBERT TREAT PAINE.
ELBRIDGE GERRY.

CONNECTICUT.
ROGER SHERMAN.
SAMUEL HUNTINGTON.
WILLIAM WILLIAMS.
OLIVER WOLCOTT.

NEW JERSEY.
RICHARD STOCKTON.
JOHN WITHERSPOON.
FRANCIS HOPKINSON.
JOHN HART.
ABRAHAM CLARK.

PENNSYLVANIA.
ROBERT MORRIS.
BENJAMIN RUSH.
BENJAMIN FRANKLIN.
JOHN MORTON.
GEORGE CLYMER.
JAMES SMITH.

PENNSYLVANIA.
GEORGE TAYLOR.
JAMES WILSON.
GEORGE ROSS.

DELAWARE.
CAESAR RODNEY.
GEORGE READ.
THOMAS M'KEAN.

MARYLAND.
SAMUEL CHASE.
WILLIAM PACA.
THOMAS STONE.
CHARLES CARROLL,
of Carrollton.

VIRGINIA.
GEORGE WYTHE.
RICHARD HENRY LEE.
THOMAS JEFFERSON.
BENJAMIN HARRISON.
THOMAS NELSON, JUN.
FRANCIS LIGHTFOOT LEE.
CARTER BRAXTON.

NORTH CAROLINA.
WILLIAM HOOPER.
JOSEPH HEWES.
JOHN PENN.

SOUTH CAROLINA.
EDWARD RUTLEDGE.
THOMAS HEYWARD, JUN.
THOMAS LYNCH, JUN.
ARTHUR MIDDLETON.

GEORGIA.
BUTTON GWINNETT.
LYMAN HALL.
GEORGE WALTON.

Immediately after the Declaration was agreed to, the Congress passed the following resolution: "Resolved, That copies of the Declaration be sent to the several assemblies, conventions, and committees or councils of safety, and to the several commanding officers of the Continental troops; that it be proclaimed in each of the United States, and at the head of the army."[4]

This celebrated instrument, says an eminent American jurist,[5] regarded as a legislative proceeding, was the solemn enactment, by the representatives of all the colonies, of a complete dissolution of their allegiance to the British crown. It severed the political connection between the people of this country and the people of England, and at once erected the different colonies into free and independent States. The body by which this step was taken constituted the actual government of the nation, at the time, and its members had been directly invested with competent legislative power to take it, and had also been specially instructed to do so. The consequences flowing from its adoption were, that the local allegiance of the inhabitants of each colony became transferred and due to the colony itself, or, as it was expressed by the Congress, became due to the laws of the colony, from which they derived protection;[6] that the people of the country became thenceforth the rightful sovereign of the country; that they became united in a national capacity, as one people; that they could thereafter enter into treaties and contract alliances with foreign nations, could levy war and conclude peace, and do all other acts pertaining to

---

[4]Journal Cong., Vol. I, p. 396.
[5]Curtis, "Constitutional History of the United States."
[6]Journal Cong., Vol. II, p. 216.

the exercise of a national sovereignty; and, finally, that, in their national capacity, they became known and designated as the United States of America. This Declaration was the first national state paper in which these words were used as the style and title of the nation. In the enacting part of the instrument the Congress styled themselves "the representatives of the United States of America in General Congress assembled;" and from that period the previously "United Colonies" have been known as a political community, both within their own borders and by the other nations of the world, by the title which they then assumed.[7]

CHAPTER III.

THE ARTICLES OF CONFEDERATION.

SKETCH OF THE ORIGIN OF THE ARTICLES—TEXT OF THE ARTICLES.

The colonies having united to obtain their rights as English subjects, when by the Declaration of Independence they became "free and independent States," they saw the necessity of continuing that union, in order to carry forward the work of independence to a completion by the agency of war, which, by the act of the king and ministry of England, was upon them.

[7] The title of "The United States of America" was formally assumed in the Articles of Confederation, when they came to be adopted. But it was in use, without formal enactment, from the date of the adoption of the Declaration of Independence.

It was now that "state sovereignty," the bane
of our national life, first manifested itself. The
States were not only jealous of each other, but they
were jealous of the formation of any outside or
over-government, which should exercise jurisdiction and power over them for the good of all; and
it became at once an ever-present cause of embar-
rassment to the Continental Congress in carrying
on the war, and in forming a general government
and a union by a written constitution.

At this time the idea of forming a strong national government by the people of the United
States in their sovereign capacity, as the rightful
possessors of all political power, it would seem,
had not entered the minds of the men of that day;
or, at least, if it had, they did not manifest it at
this time. They looked only to the formation of a
league or federal alliance between the thirteen
independent and sovereign States in their corporate capacities. They had to be driven to the
formation of a strong national government, by the
people, by an absolute necessity to preserve their
existence as a nation, and to promote the welfare
and happiness of the people, and secure the blessings of liberty to themselves and their posterity.
Indeed, the building of the new Republic had to be
gradually evolved, for there were no precedents to
guide them in carrying out the principles of the
Declaration of Independence.

The Continental Congress, therefore, on June
11, 1776, resolved that a committee should be appointed to prepare, and properly digest, a form

of confederation to be entered into by the several States. This committee consisted of one delegate from each State, and John Dickenson, of Pennsylvania, was chosen its chairman.[8] On the 12th of July the committee reported to Congress a draft of Articles of Confederation. From that time until the 20th of August daily debates were had upon the articles, when the report was laid aside, and was not again taken up for consideration until the 8th of April, 1777. In the meanwhile several of the States, in accordance with the recommendation of the Congress, had adopted Constitutions, republican in form, for their respective government, and Congress was practically acknowledged the supreme head in all matters appertaining to the war then going on. It emitted bills of credit, or paper money, appointed foreign ministers, and opened negotiations with foreign governments. But the government thus carried on was revolutionary in its nature, and continued so until the Articles of Confederation were adopted by the State Legislatures of the several States.

From the 8th of April until the 15th of November following, the articles were debated two or three times a week and several amendments were made. As the confederation might be a permanent bond of union, says one, of course local interests were considered prospectively. If the union had been designed to be temporary, to meet the exigencies arising from the state of war in

---

[8]The committee consisted of Messrs. Bartlett, Samuel Adams, Hopkins, Sherman, R. R. Livingston, Dickenson, McKean, Stone, Nelson, Hewes, Edward Rutledge, and Gwinnett.

which the States then were, local questions could hardly have had weight enough to have elicited debate; but such was not the case, and of course the wise men who were then in Congress looked beyond the present, and endeavored to act accordingly.

From the 7th of October, 1777, until the 15th of November of that year, the debates upon the subject were almost daily, and the conflicting interests of the several States were strongly brought into view by the speakers. On the 15th day of November, 1777, the Articles of Confederation were adopted; and on the 17th Congress transmitted from Yorktown, where it was then in session, authenticated copies of the same to the Legislatures of the several States for their ratification, accompanied by the following

CIRCULAR LETTER:

"Congress having agreed upon a plan of confederacy for securing the freedom, sovereignty, and independence of the United States, authentic copies are now transmitted for the consideration of the respective Legislatures.

"This business, equally intricate and important, has in its progress been attended with uncommon embarrassments and delay, which the most anxious solicitude and persevering diligence could not prevent. To form a permanent union, accommodated to the opinion and wishes of the delegates of so many States differing in habits, produce, commerce, and internal police, was found to be a work which nothing but time and reflection, conspiring with a disposition to conciliate, could mature and accomplish.

"Hardly is it to be expected that any plan, in the variety of provisions essential to our union, should exactly correspond with the maxims and political views of every particular State. Let it be remarked that, after the most careful inquiry and the fullest information, this is proposed as the best which could be adapted to the circumstances of all, and as that alone which affords any tolerable prospect of general satisfaction.

"Permit us, then, earnestly to recommend these articles to the immediate and dispassionate attention of the legislatures of the respective States. Let them be candidly reviewed, under a sense of the difficulty of combining in one general system the various sentiments and interests of a continent divided into so many sovereign and independent communities, under a conviction of the absolute necessity of uniting all our counsels and all our strength to maintain and defend our common liberties; let them be examined with a liberality becoming brethren and fellow citizens surrounded by the same imminent dangers, contending for the same illustrious prize, and deeply interested in being forever bound and connected together by ties the most intimate and indissoluble; and, finally, let them be adjusted with the temper and magnanimity of wise and patriotic legislators who, while they are concerned for the prosperity of their own more immediate circle, are capable of rising superior to local attachments when they may be incompatible with the safety, happiness, and glory of the general confederacy.

"We have reason to regret the time which has elapsed in preparing this plan for consideration; with additional solicitude we look forward to that which must be necessarily spent before it can be ratified. Every motive loudly calls upon us to hasten its conclusion.

"More than any other consideration, it will confound our foreign enemies, defeat the flagitious practices of the disaffected, strengthen and confirm our friends, support our public credit, restore the value of our money, enable us to maintain our fleets and armies, and add weight and respect to our counsels at home and to our treaties abroad.

"In short, this salutary measure can no longer be deferred. It seems essential to our very existence as a free people, and without it we may feel constrained to bid adieu to independence, to liberty and safety—blessings which, from the justice of our cause and the favor of our Almighty Creator visibly manifested in our protection, we have reason to expect, if, in an humble dependence on His divine providence, we strenuously exert the means which are placed in our power.

"To conclude, if the legislature of any State shall not be assembled, Congress recommend to the executive authority to convene it without delay; and to each respective legislature it is recommended to invest its delegates with competent powers ultimately, in the name and behalf of the

State, to subscribe Articles of Confederation and Perpetual Union of the United States; and to attend Congress for that purpose on or before the tenth day of March next."

Notwithstanding this earnest and patriotic appeal of Congress to the thirteen States, recommending that they ratify the Articles of Confederation, at an early day, they were destined to remain unratified for several years. Much opposition was made to them in all the States. Their ratification was commenced on the 9th of July, 1778; but it was not completed until the 1st day of March, 1781.

The principal reason for this long delay was the claim made by some of the States to the vast unoccupied western territory—extending to the Mississippi River. Their conflicting claims to this territory formed one of the chief obstacles to a general union of the States under the Articles of Confederation. Those States, whose colonial charters gave them no claim to any part of this territory, insisted that the other States, which laid claims to it under their charters, should surrender their claims to the United States, for the use and benefit of all the States. Impoverished as the States then were, and overburdened with debts contracted for the general good of the whole, it was reasonably claimed that this vacant territory, so unequally distributed originally, ought to be made a common fund for defraying the expenses of the war.[9]

_____
[9]Walker's "American Law."

13

Seven States laid claim to an interest in this vacant territory. These were the States of Massachusetts, Connecticut, New York, Virginia, North Carolina, South Carolina, and Georgia; four of these—New York, Connecticut, Massachusetts, and Virginia—claimed the territory Northwest of the Ohio River to the Mississippi; Virginia claiming the greater portion of it.

But so little was known of our topography when the grants were made to the different colonies—by Great Britain—that, besides being vague and often contradictory, some of them were highly extravagant in point of quantity. For example, the descriptive words in the grant to Virginia, covered a tract four hundred miles in width, and extending in terms from the Atlantic to the Pacific Ocean. The grant to Connecticut was of a similar character, and the rest not greatly different. The consequence was that immediately after the Declaration of Independence, conflicting claims to territory were set up by the several States, which threatened to prevent the formation of a permanent union.[10]

Maryland made a vigorous and special objection to agreeing to the Articles until some provision should be made for the cession of the western lands to the United States, for the benefit of all the States. Her legislature in the instructions to her delegates in Congress, refusing to ratify the Articles unless this was done, among other things, said:

[10]Walker's "American Law."

"Although the pressure of immediate calamities, the dread of their continuance from the appearance of disunion, and some other peculiar circumstances, may have induced some States to accede to the present Confederation, contrary to their own interests and judgments, it requires no great share of foresight to predict that, when those causes cease to operate, the States which have thus acceded to the Confederation will consider it as no longer binding, and will eagerly embrace the first occasion of asserting their just rights, and securing their independence. Is it possible that those States who are ambitiously grasping at territories to which, in our judgment, they have not the least shadow of exclusive right, will use with greater moderation the increase of wealth and power derived from those territories, when acquired, than what they have displayed in their endeavors to acquire them? We think not. We are convinced the same spirit which hath prompted them to insist on a claim so extravagant, so repugnant to every principle of justice, so incompatible with the general welfare of all the States, will urge them on to add oppression to injustice. If they should not be incited by a superiority of wealth and strength to oppress by open force their less wealthy and less powerful neighbors, yet depopulation, and consequently the impoverishment, of those States will necessarily follow, which, by an unfair construction of the Confederation, may be stripped of a common interest, and the common benefits derivable from the Western Country. Sup-

pose, for instance, Virginia indisputably possessed
of the extensive and fertile country to which she
has set up a claim, what would be the probable
consequences to Maryland of such an undisturbed
and undisputed possession? They cannot escape
the least discerning.

"Virginia, by selling on the most moderate
terms a small proportion of the lands in question,
would draw into her treasury vast sums of money;
and in proportion to the sums arising from such
sales would be enabled to lessen her taxes. Lands
comparatively cheap, and taxes comparatively
low, with the lands and taxes of an adjacent State,
would quickly drain the State thus disadvantage-
ously circumstanced of its most useful inhabitants;
its wealth and its consequence in the scale of the
confederated States would sink of course. A claim
so injurious to more than one-half, if not the whole,
of the United States, ought to be supported by the
clearest evidence of the right. Yet what evidences
of that right have been produced? What arguments alleged in support either of the evidences
or the right? None that we have heard of deserv-
ing a serious refutation.   *   *   *

"We are convinced, policy and justice require,
that a country unsettled at the commencement of
this war, claimed by the British crown, and ceded
to it by the treaty of Paris, if wrested from the
common enemy by the blood and treasure of the
thirteen States, should be considered as a common
property, subject to be parcelled out by Congress
into free, convenient, and independent govern-

ments, in such manner and at such times as the wisdom of that assembly shall hereafter direct.

"Thus convinced, we should betray the trust reposed in us by our constituents, were we to authorize you to ratify, on their behalf, the Confederation, unless it be further explained. We have coolly and dispassionately considered the subject; we have weighed probable inconveniences and hardships against the sacrifice of just and essential rights; and do instruct you not to agree to the Confederation, unless an article or articles be added thereto in conformity with our declaration. Should we succeed in obtaining such article or articles, then you are hereby fully empowered to accede to the Confederation. * * *

"Also we desire and instruct you to move, at a proper time, that these instructions be read to Congress by their Secretary, and entered on the Journals of Congress.

"We have spoken with freedom, as became freemen; and we sincerely wish that these our representations may make such an impression on that assembly as to induce them to make such addition to the Articles of Confederation as may bring about a permanent union."

On the 21st of May, 1779, the delegates of Maryland informed Congress that they have received instructions from their State legislature respecting the Articles of Confederation, which they are directed to lay before Congress, and have entered on their Journals. The instructions were read, and then referred to a committee; subsequently the committee made its report to Congress.

On the 6th day of September, 1780, Congress took into consideration the report of the committee to whom were referred the instructions of the General Assembly of Maryland to their delegates in Congress respecting the Articles of Confederation, and the declaration therein referred to; the act of the legislature of New York on the same subject; and the remonstrance of the General Assembly of Virginia, which report was agreed to, and is in the words following:

"That, having duly considered the several matters to them submitted, they conceive it unnecessary to examine into the merits or policy of the instructions or declaration of the General Assembly of Maryland, or of the remonstrance of the General Assembly of Virginia, as they involve questions a discussion of which was declined, on mature consideration, when the Articles of Confederation were debated; nor, in the opinion of the committee, can such questions be now revived with any prospect of conciliation: That it appears more advisable to press upon these States which can remove the embarrassments respecting the Western Country a liberal surrender of a portion of their territorial claims, since they cannot be preserved entire without endangering the stability of the general Confederacy; to remind them how indispensably necessary it is to establish the Federal Union on a fixed and permanent basis, and on principles acceptable to all its respective members;

how essential to public credit and confidence, to
the support of our army, to the vigor of our councils, and success of our measures, to our tranquillity at home, our reputation abroad, to our very
existence as a free, sovereign, and independent people; that we are fully persuaded the wisdom of the
respective legislatures will lead them to a full and
impartial consideration of a subject so interesting to the United States, and so necessary to the
happy establishment of the Federal Union; that
they are confirmed in these expectations by a view
of the before-mentioned act of the legislature of
New York, submitted to their consideration; that
this act is expressly calculated to accelerate the
federal alliance, by removing, as far as depends
on that State, the impediment arising from the
Western Country, and for that purpose to yield up
a portion of territorial claim for the general benefit.

"Whereupon: Resolved, That copies of the several papers referred to the committee be transmitted, with a copy of the report, to the legislatures of the several States; and that it be earnestly
recommended to these States who have claims to
the Western Country to pass such laws, and give
their delegates in Congress such powers, as may
effectually remove the only obstacle to a final ratification of the Articles of Confederation; and that
the legislature of Maryland be earnestly requested
to authorize their delegates in Congress to subscribe the said articles."

This patriotic appeal of Congress, and the example of New York in authorizing a cession of her interest in the western lands, were not in vain. The other States imitated the example of New York, and, at successive intervals, ceded to the United States—with certain reservations by some —all their claims to the Western Country.[11]

Thus by the Revolution and these cessions the United States derived their title to all that portion of the public domain north of Florida and east of the Mississippi River—a vast territory. It will be remembered that the public domain acquired by the United States subsequent to this, was obtained in a different manner; quite a large portion of it by purchase from foreign governments, and the remainder by conquest. The most of these acquisitions were, the Louisiana purchase from France, in 1803; the Florida purchase from Spain, in 1819; the Mexican cession, in 1848, by conquest of Mexico; and the Alaska purchase from Russia, in 1867.

The legislature of Maryland having received the appeal of Congress, in which she was earnestly requested to authorize her delegates in Congress to subscribe the Articles of Confederation, without waiting for the States to make cessions of their claims to the western territory, authorized, in February, 1781, her delegates in Congress to subscribe

[11]The Northwestern territory was ceded as follows: That of New York was made March 1st, 1781, under the authority of the Act of the Legislature of that State, of the 19th of February, 1780. That of Virginia was made March 1st, 1784, under the authority of an Act of the 20th of December, 1783. That of Massachusetts, on the 19th of April, 1785, under the authority of the Acts of that State, of the 13th of November, 1784, and 17th of March, 1785; and that of Connecticut, on the 14th of September, 1786, under the authority of an Act of that State of May, 1786. See Kent's Commentaries, Vol. I, pp. 271-272 (11th Ed.).

and ratify the Articles of Confederation; declaring, however, in the same act, "that, by acceding to the said Confederation, this State doth not relinquish, or intend to relinquish, any right or interest she hath with the other united or Confederated States to the back country; but claims the same as fully as was done by the legislature of this State in their declaration which stands entered on the Journals of Congress; this State relying on the justice of the several States hereafter, as to the said claim made by this State." Whereupon the Articles were signed and ratified by John Hanson and Daniel Carroll, her delegates, on the 1st day of March, 1781. The Articles of Confederation were now in full force and effect, and so continued until the 4th day of March, 1789, when the Constitution of the United States went into effect.

It was well that Maryland insisted, with so much vigor and with such justness of right, that she would not ratify the Articles of Confederation unless some provision was made for the States claiming interests in the western territory for ceding their claims to the United States, for the benefit of all the States. For it is quite certain that her action and delay in ratifying the Articles, caused a cession of that territory to the United States, preserved the Union, and, as Virginia claimed a large portion of the North Western Territory, prevented slavery from being fastened on it, which it is probable would have been done had Virginia retained her interest therein. Thus the free States would have been hemmed in, and the development of freedom prevented. But Providence determined the course of events otherwise; and that Territory was dedicated to freedom.

The following is the text of the

ARTICLES OF CONFEDERATION.

To all to whom these presents shall come,

We, the undersigned, delegates of the States affixed to our names, send greeting:

Whereas the delegates of the United States of America in Congress assembled did, on the fifteenth day of November, in the year of our Lord one thousand seven hundred and seventy-seven, and in the second year of the independence of America, agree to certain Articles of Confederation and Perpetual Union between the States of New Hampshire, Massachusetts Bay, Rhode Island and Providence Plantations, Connecticut, New York, New Jersey, Pennsylvania, Delaware, Maryland, Virginia, North Carolina, South Carolina, and Georgia, in the words following, viz.:

Articles of Confederation and Perpetual Union between the States of New Hampshire, Massachusetts Bay, Rhode Island and Providence Plantations, Connecticut, New York, New Jersey, Pennsylvania, Delaware, Maryland, Virginia, North Carolina, South Carolina, and Georgia.

Article I. The style of this Confederacy shall be, "The United States of America."

Article II. Each State retains its sovereignty, freedom, and independence, and every power, jurisdiction, and right, which is not by this Confederation expressly delegated to the United States in Congress assembled.

Article III. The said States hereby severally enter into a firm league of friendship with each other for their common defense, the security of their liberties, and their mutual and general welfare; binding themselves to assist each other against all force offered to, or attacks made upon them, or any of them, on account of religion, sovereignty, trade, or any other pretense whatever.

Article IV. The better to secure and perpetuate mutual friendship and intercourse among the people of the different States in this Union, the free inhabitants of each of these States, paupers, vagabonds, and fugitives from justice excepted, shall be entitled to all privileges and immunities of free citizens in the several States; and the people of each State shall have free ingress and regress to and from any other State, and shall enjoy therein all the privileges of trade and commerce, subject to the same duties, impositions, and restrictions, as the inhabitants thereof respectively: Provided, That such restrictions, shall not extend so far as to prevent the removal of property imported into any State to any other State, of which the owner is an inhabitant: Provided, also, That no imposition, duties, or restriction shall be laid by any State on the property of the United States or either of them.

If any person guilty of or charged with treason, felony, or other high misdemeanor, in any State, shall flee from justice, and be found in any of the

United States, he shall, upon demand of the governor or executive power of the State from which he fled, be delivered up, and removed to the State having jurisdiction of his offense.

Full faith and credit shall be given in each of these States to the records, acts, and judicial proceedings of the courts and magistrates of every other State.

Article V. For the more convenient management of the general interests of the United States, delegates shall be annually appointed in such manner as the Legislature of each State shall direct, to meet in Congress on the first Monday in November, in every year, with a power reserved to each State to recall its delegates or any of them, at any time within the year, and to send others in their stead for the remainder of the year.

No State shall be represented in Congress by less than two nor by more than seven members; and no person shall be capable of being a delegate for more than three years in any term of six years; nor shall any person, being a delegate, be capable of holding any office under the United States, for which he, or another for his benefit, receives any salary, fees or emolument of any kind.

Each State shall maintain its own delegates in a meeting of the States, and while they act as members of the committee of these States.

In determining questions in the United States in Congress assembled, each State shall have one vote.

Freedom of speech and debate in Congress shall

not be impeached or questioned in any court or place out of Congress; and the members of Congress shall be protected in their persons from arrests and imprisonments during the time of their going to and from, and attendance on, Congress, except for treason, felony, or breach of the peace.

Article VI. No State, without the consent of the United States in Congress assembled, shall send any embassy to, or receive any embassy from, or enter into any conference, agreement, alliance, or treaty with any King, prince, or state; nor shall any person holding any office of profit or trust under the United States, or any of them, accept of any present, emolument, office or title of any kind whatever from any King, prince, or foreign state; nor shall the United States in Congress assembled, or any of them, grant any title of nobility.

No two or more States shall enter into any treaty, confederation, or alliance whatever between them without the consent of the United States in Congress assembled, specifying accurately the purposes for which the same is to be entered into, and how long it shall continue.

No State shall lay any imposts or duties, which may interfere with any stipulations in treaties entered into by the United States in Congress assembled with any King, prince, or state, in pursuance of any treaties already proposed by Congress to the Courts of France and Spain.

No vessels of war shall be kept up in time of peace by any State, except such number only as shall be deemed necessary by the United States

in Congress assembled, for the defense of such
State, or its trade; nor shall any body of forces be
kept up by any State in time of peace, except such
number only, as, in the judgment of the United
States, in Congress assembled, shall be deemed requisite to garrison the forts necessary for the defense of such State; but every State shall always
keep up a well regulated and disciplined militia,
sufficiently armed and accoutered, and shall provide and constantly have ready for use, in public
stores, a due number of field-pieces and tents, and
a proper quantity of arms, ammunition, and camp
equipage.

No State shall engage in any war without the
consent of the United States in Congress assembled,
unless such State be actually invaded by enemies,
or shall have received certain advice of a resolution being formed by some nation of Indians to in-
vade such State, and the danger is so imminent
as not to admit of a delay till the United States in
Congress assembled can be consulted; nor shall
any State grant commissions to any ships or vessels of war, nor letters of marque or reprisal, except it be after a declaration of war by the United
States in Congress assembled; and then only
against the kingdom or state, and the subjects
thereof, against which war has been so declared,
and under such regulations as shall be established
by the United States in Congress assembled, unless such State be infested by pirates, in which
case vessels of war may be fitted out for that occasion, and kept so long as the danger shall con-

tinue, or until the United States in Congress assembled shall determine otherwise.

Article VII. When land forces are raised by any State for the common defense, all officers of, or under the rank of colonel, shall be appointed by the Legislature of each State respectively by whom such forces shall be raised, or in such manner as such State shall direct; and all vacancies shall be filled up by the State which first made the appointment.

Article VIII. All charges of war, and all other expenses that shall be incurred for the common defense or general welfare and allowed by the United States in Congress assembled, shall be defrayed out of a common treasury, which shall be supplied by the several States, in proportion to the value of all land within each State, granted to, or surveyed for, any person, as such land and the buildings and improvements thereon shall be estimated, according to such mode as the United States in Congress assembled shall, from time to time, direct and appoint.

The taxes for paying that proportion shall be laid and levied by the authority and direction of the Legislatures of the several States, within the time agreed upon by the United States in Congress assembled.

Article IX. The United States in Congress assembled shall have the sole and exclusive right and power of determining on peace and war, except in the cases mentioned in the sixth article; of sending and receiving embassadors; entering into treaties and alliances: Provided, That no treaty of commerce shall be made whereby the legislative power of the respective States shall be restrained from imposing such imposts and duties on foreigners as their own people are subjected to, or from prohibiting the exportation or importation of any species of goods or commodities whatsoever; of establishing rules for deciding, in all cases, what captures on land or water shall be legal, and in what manner prizes taken by land or naval forces in the service of the United States, shall be divided or appropriated; of granting letters of marque and reprisal in times of peace; appointing courts for the trial of piracies and felonies committed on the high seas, and establishing courts for receiving and determining finally, appeals in all cases of captures: Provided, That no member of Congress shall be appointed a judge of any of the said courts.

The United States in Congress assembled shall also be the last resort on appeal in all disputes and differences now subsisting, or that hereafter may arise between two or more States concerning boundary, jurisdiction, or any other cause whatever; which authority shall always be exercised in the manner following: Whenever the legislative or executive authority or lawful agent of any State in controversy with another, shall present a petition to Congress, stating the matter in question, and praying for a hearing, notice thereof shall be given by order of Congress to the legislative or executive authority of the other State in controversy, and a day assigned for the appearance of

the parties by their lawful agents, who shall then
be directed to appoint, by joint consent, commissioners or judges to constitute a court for hearing
and determining the matter in question; but if
they cannot agree, Congress shall name three persons out of each of the United States, and from the
list of such persons each party shall alternately
strike out one, the petitioners beginning, until the
number shall be reduced to thirteen; and from that
number not less than seven nor more than nine
names, as Congress shall direct, shall, in the presence of Congress, be drawn out by lot; and the
persons whose names shall be so drawn, or any
five of them, shall be commissioners or judges, to
hear and finally determine the controversy, so always as a major part of the judges who shall hear
the cause, shall agree in the determination; and
if either party shall neglect to attend at the day
appointed, without showing reasons which Congress shall judge sufficient, or, being present, shall
refuse to strike, the Congress shall proceed to nominate three persons out of each State, and the Secretary of Congress shall strike in behalf of such
party absent or refusing; and the judgment and
sentence of the court to be appointed in the manner before prescribed shall be final and conclusive;
and if any of the parties shall refuse to submit to
the authority of such court or to appear or defend
their claim or cause, the court shall, nevertheless,
proceed to pronounce sentence or judgment, which
shall, in like manner, be final and decisive; the
judgment or sentence, and other proceedings, being

14

in either case transmitted to Congress, and lodged among the acts of Congress for the security of the parties concerned: Provided, That every commissioner, before he sits in judgment, shall take an oath, to be administered by one of the judges of the supreme or superior court of the State, where the cause shall be tried, "well and truly to hear and determine the matter in question, according to the best of his judgment without favor, affection, or hope of reward": Provided, also, That no State shall be deprived of territory for the benefit of the United States.

All controversies concerning the private right of soil claimed under different grants of two or more States, whose jurisdictions, as they may respect such lands, and the States which passed such grants, are adjusted, the said grants or either of them being at the same time claimed to have originated antecedent to such settlement of jurisdiction, shall, on the petition of either party to the Congress of the United States, be finally determined, as near as may be, in the same manner as is before prescribed for deciding disputes respecting territorial jurisdiction between different States.

The United States in Congress assembled shall also have the sole and exclusive right and power of regulating the alloy and value of coin struck by their own authority, or by that of the respective States; fixing the standard of weights and measures throughout the United States; regulating the trade and managing all affairs with the Indians, not members of any of the States: Provided, That

the legislative right of any State within its own
limits, be not infringed or violated; establishing
and regulating post-offices from one State to another, throughout all the United States, and exact-
ing such postage on the papers passing through
the same, as may be requisite to defray the expenses of the said office; appointing all officers of
the land forces in the service of the United States,
excepting regimental officers; appointing all the
officers of the naval forces, and commissioning all
officers whatever in the service of the United
States; making rules for the government and regulation of the said land and naval forces, and directing their operations.

The United States in Congress assembled shall
have authority to appoint a committee to sit in
the recess of Congress, to be denominated "a Committee of the States," and to consist of one delegate from each State, and to appoint such other
committees and civil officers as may be necessary
for managing the general affairs of the United
States, under their direction; to appoint one of
their number to preside; provided that no person
be allowed to serve in the office of president more
than one year in any term of three years; to ascertain the necessary sums of money to be raised for
the service of the United States, and to appropriate
and apply the same for defraying the public expenses; to borrow money or emit bills on the credit
of the United States, transmitting every half year
to the respective States, an account of the sums
of money so borrowed or emitted; to build and

equip a navy; to agree upon the number of land
forces, and to make requisitions from each State
for its quota, in proportion to the number of white
inhabitants in such State, which requisitions shall
be binding; and thereupon the Legislature of each
State shall appoint the regimental officers, raise
the men, and clothe, arm, and equip them in a
soldier-like manner, at the expense of the United
States; and the officers and men so clothed, armed,
and equipped, shall march to the place appointed,
and within the time agreed on by the United States
in Congress assembled; but if the United States in
Congress assembled shall, on consideration of circumstances, judge proper that any State should
not raise men, or should raise a smaller number
than its quota, and that any other State should
raise a greater number of men than the quota
thereof, such extra number shall be raised, offi-
cered, clothed, armed, and equipped in the same
manner as the quota of each State, unless the Legislature of such State shall judge that such extra
number cannot be safely spared out of the same;
in which case they shall raise, officer, clothe, arm,
and equip as many of such extra number as they
judge can be safely spared. And the officers and
men so clothed, armed, and equipped shall march
to the place appointed, and within the time agreed
on by the United States in Congress assembled.

The United States in Congress assembled shall
never engage in a war, nor grant letters of marque
and reprisal in time of peace, nor enter into any
treaties or alliances, nor coin money, nor regulate

the value thereof, nor ascertain the sums and expenses necessary for the defense and welfare of the United States or any of them, nor emit bills, nor borrow money on the credit of the United States, nor appropriate money, nor agree upon the number of vessels of war to be built or purchased, or the number of land or sea forces to be raised, nor appoint a commander-in-chief of the Army or Navy, unless nine States assent to the same; nor shall a question on any other point, except for adjourning from day to day, be determined, unless by the votes of a majority of the United States in Congress assembled.

The Congress of the United States shall have power to adjourn to any time within the year, and to any place within the United States, so that no period of adjournment be for a longer duration than the space of six months; and shall publish the Journal of their proceedings monthly, except such parts thereof relating to treaties, alliances, or military operations, as in their judgment require secrecy; and the yeas and nays of the delegates of each State on any question, shall be entered on the Journal, when it is desired by any delegate; and the delegates of a State, or any of them, at his or their request, shall be furnished with a transcript of the said Journal, except such parts as are above excepted, to lay before the Legislature of the several States.

Article X. The Committee of the States, or any nine of them, shall be authorized to execute, in the recess of Congress, such of the powers of Congress as the United States in Congress assembled, by the consent of nine States, shall, from time to time, think expedient to vest them with: Provided, That no power be delegated to the said committee, for the exercise of which, by the Articles of Confederation, the voice of nine States in the Congress of the United States assembled is requisite.

Article XI. Canada, acceding to this confederation, and joining in the measures of the United States, shall be admitted into, and entitled to, all the advantages of this Union; but no other colony shall be admitted into the same, unless such admission be agreed to by nine States.

Article XII. All bills of credit emitted, moneys borrowed, and debts contracted, by or under the authority of Congress, before the assembling of the United States, in pursuance of the present confederation, shall be deemed and considered as a charge against the United States, for payment and satisfaction whereof the said United States and the public faith are hereby solemnly pledged.

Article XIII. Every State shall abide by the determinations of the United States in Congress assembled, on all questions which by this confederation are submitted to them. And the articles of this confederation shall be inviolably observed by every State, and the union shall be perpetual; nor shall any alteration at any time hereafter be made in any of them, unless such alteration be agreed to in a Congress of the United States, and be afterwards confirmed by the Legislatures of every State.

And whereas it has pleased the Great Governor of the World to incline the hearts of the Legislatures we respectively represent in Congress, to approve of, and to authorize us to ratify the said articles of confederation and perpetual union: Know ye, That we, the undersigned delegates, by virtue of the power and authority to us given for that purpose, do, by these presents, in the name and in behalf of our respective constituents, fully and entirely ratify and confirm each and every of the said Articles of Confederation and Perpetual Union, and all and singular the matters and things therein contained. And we do further solemnly plight and engage the faith of our respective constituents, that they shall abide by the determinations of the United States, in Congress assembled, on all questions which, by the said confederation, are submitted to them; and that the articles thereof shall be inviolably observed by the States we respectively represent; and that the union shall be perpetual.

In Witness Whereof we have hereunto set our hands, in Congress. Done at Philadelphia, in the State of Pennsylvania, the ninth day of July, in the year of our Lord one thousand seven hundred and seventy-eight, and in the third year of the Independence of America.

On the part and behalf of the State of New Hampshire.—Josiah Bartlett, John Wentworth, Jr., August 8, 1778.

On the part and behalf of the State of Massachusetts Bay.—John Hancock, Samuel Adams, Elbridge Gerry, Francis Dana, James Lovell, Samuel Holten.

On the part and in behalf of the State of Rhode Island and Providence Plantations.—William Ellery, Henry Marchant, John Collins.

On the part and behalf of the State of Connecticut.—Roger Sherman, Samuel Huntington, Oliver Wolcott, Titus Hosmer, Andrew Adams.

On the part and behalf of the State of New York.—Jas. Duane, Fra. Lewis, Wm. Duer, Gouv. Morris.

On the part and in behalf of the State of New Jersey.—Jno. Witherspoon, Nath. Scudder, Nov. 26, 1778.

On the part and behalf of the State of Pennsylvania.—Robt. Morris, Daniel Roberdeau, Jona. Bayard Smith, William Clingan, Joseph Reed, July 22d, 1778.

On the part and behalf of the State of Delaware.—Thos. McKean, Feb. 13, 1779, John Dickinson, May 5, 1779, Nicholas Van Dyke.

On the part and behalf of the State of Maryland.—John Hanson, March 1, 1781, Daniel Carroll, March 1, 1781.

On the part and behalf of the State of Virginia. —Richard Henry Lee, John Banister, Thomas Adams, Jno. Harvie, Francis Lightfoot Lee.

On the part and behalf of the State of North Carolina.—John Penn, July 21, 1778, Corns. Harnett, Jno. Williams.

On the part and behalf of the State of South Carolina.—Henry Laurens, William Henry Drayton, Jno. Mathews, Richard Hutson, Thomas Heyward, Jr.

On the part and behalf of the State of Georgia. —Jno. Walton, July 24, 1778, Edw. Telfair, Edw. Langworthy.

CHAPTER IV.

THE ORDINANCE OF 1787.

SKETCH OF THE ORIGIN OF THE ORDINANCE.—TEXT OF THE ORDINANCE.

The United States acquired by the Revolution, and by cessions of New York, Connecticut, Massachusetts, and Virginia, all the vast unsettled territory North West of the River Ohio, bounded by the Great Lakes on the north and the Mississippi River on the west. It now became necessary, as emigration was moving westward and the people were desirous of settling in that territory, and of creating new States out of it, to make some provision for the government of the same; and to provide for the admission, into the Union, of the States which might be carved out of it.

The Articles of Confederation did not give Congress power to provide for the government of territory acquired by the United States, nor for the admission of new States into the Union. Congress, however, out of the necessities of the case, assumed the right to legislate for the Northwestern Territory in enacting a constitution for its government,

and providing therein for the admission of States
which might be organized out of the same. Their
labors resulted in what is called the "Ordinance
of 1787."

This ordinance was an instrument of great
value. It laid down principles so just and wise
as to be accepted by future legislators as a model
in the preliminary organization of all the other
States admitted into the Union.

History says, that some of its provisions formed
part of a political compromise between the free
and slave States of great importance. The introduction of slavery into Virginia, in 1620, proved
fruitful of dangers and disasters to American liberty. Moral, social and industrial antagonisms
gradually sprung out of it and threatened the peace
and stability of the Union from its beginning. The
instinctive foresight of danger, the causes of which
they could not agree to banish altogether, led the
founders of the Republic to compare interests and
views and ascertain what settlement of them was
possible. Collision, apparently, would be fatal;
union was indispensable; therefore they made
terms with each other, giving the territory north
of the Ohio to the free labor system, and that south
of the Ohio to the forced or slave labor system.[12]
The situation immediately after the Revolution
seemed too critical to allow a violent contest, and
neither the principles nor the interests involved
were sufficiently well developed at that time to
impress those great men with the danger which a

---

[12]For some effects of the compromise, see Chap. IV. of Part I,
Book I.

compromise might involve. Other dangers seemed
to them more immediate.

Each period of national history has its own
measure of wisdom and foresight, its special questions to settle, and its instinct of self-preservation.
The compromises, with relation to slavery, involved
in the Ordinance of 1787, and in the Constitution
of the United States adopted about two months
later, by the Convention at Philadelphia, may be
accepted, when all the circumstances and difficulties of that period are weighed, as a proof of the
patriotic wisdom and moderation of the Fathers
of the Republic.[13]

The following is the full text of the

ORDINANCE OF 1787.

An Ordinance for the Government of the Territory of the United States Northwest of the Ohio
River. (In Congress, July 13, 1787.)

Be it ordained by the United States in Congress
assembled, That the said Territory, for the purposes of temporary government, be one district;
subject, however, to be divided into two districts,
as future circumstances may, in the opinion of Congress, make it expedient.

Be it ordained by the authority aforesaid, That the estates both of resident and
non-resident proprietors in the said Territory,
dying intestate, shall descend to and be distributed among their children, and the descendants of a deceased child, in equal parts;

---

[13]Walker's "The Mississippi Valley."

the descendants of a deceased child or grandchild
to take the share of their deceased parent in equal
parts among them; and where there shall be no
children or descendants, then in equal parts to the
next of kin, in equal degree; and among collater-
als, the children of a deceased brother or sister
of the intestate shall have, in equal parts among
them, their deceased parents' share; and there
shall, in no case, be a distinction between kindred
of the whole and half blood; saving in all cases to
the widow of the intestate, her third part of the
real estate for life, and one-third part of the personal estate; and this law relative to descents and
dower shall remain in full force until altered by
the Legislature of the district. And until the governor and judges shall adopt laws as hereinafter
mentioned, estates in the said Territory may be
devised or bequeathed by wills in writing, signed
and sealed by him or her, in whom the estate may
be, (being of full age,) and attested by three witnesses; and real estates may be conveyed by lease
and release, or bargain and sale, signed, sealed, and
delivered by the person, being of full age, in whom
the estate may be and attested by two witnesses,
provided such wills be duly proved, and such con-
veyances be acknowledged, or the execution thereof duly proved and be recorded within one year,
after proper magistrates, courts, and registers
shall be appointed for that purpose; and personal
property may be transferred by delivery, saving,
however, to the French and Canadian inhabitants,
and other settlers of the Kaskaskies, Saint Vin-

cent's, and the neighboring villages, who have heretofore professed themselves citizens of Virginia, their laws and customs now in force among them, relative to the descent and conveyance of property.

Be it ordained by the authority aforesaid, That there shall be appointed, from time to time, by Congress, a governor, whose commission shall continue in force for the term of three years, unless sooner revoked by Congress; he shall reside in the district, and have a freehold estate therein, in one thousand acres of land, while in the exercise of his office.

There shall be appointed, from time to time, by Congress, a secretary, whose commission shall continue in force for four years, unless sooner revoked; he shall reside in the district, and have a freehold estate therein, in five hundred acres of land, while in the exercise of his office; it shall be his duty to keep and preserve the acts and laws passed by the Legislature, and the public records of the district, and the proceedings of the governor in his executive department; and transmit authentic copies of such acts and proceedings every six months to the secretary of Congress. There shall also be appointed a court, to consist of three judges, any two of whom to form a court, who shall have a common law jurisdiction, and reside in the district, and have each therein a freehold estate, in five hundred acres of land, while in the exercise of their offices, and their commissions shall continue in force during good behavior.

The governor and judges, or a majority of them, shall adopt and publish in the district such laws of the original States, criminal and civil, as may be necessary, and best suited to the circumstances of the district, and report them to Congress, from time to time, which laws shall be in force in the district until the organization of the general assembly therein, unless disapproved of by Congress; but afterwards the Legislature shall have authority to alter them as they shall think fit.

The governor for the time being shall be commander-in-chief of the militia; appoint and commission all officers in the same below the rank of general officers. All general officers shall be appointed and commissioned by Congress.

Previous to the organization of the General Assembly, the governor shall appoint such magistrates and other civil officers in each county or township as he shall find necessary for the preservation of the peace and good order in the same. After the General Assembly shall be organized, the powers and duties of magistrates and other civil officers shall be regulated and defined by the said assembly; but all magistrates and other civil officers, not herein otherwise directed, shall, during the continuance of this temporary government, be appointed by the governor.

For the prevention of crimes and injuries, the laws to be adopted or made shall have force in all parts of the district, and for the execution of process, criminal and civil, the governor shall make proper divisions thereof; and he shall proceed from time to time, as circumstances may require, to lay out the parts of the district in which the Indian titles shall have been extinguished, into counties and townships, subject, however, to such alterations as may thereafter be made by the Legislature.

So soon as there shall be five thousand free male inhabitants of full age in the district, upon giving proof thereof to the governor, they shall receive authority, with time and place, to elect representatives from their counties or townships, to represent them in the General Assembly: Provided, That for every five hundred free male inhabitants, there shall be one representative; and so on, progressively, with the number of free male inhabitants, shall the right of representation increase, until the number of representatives shall amount to twenty-five; after which the number and proportion of representatives shall be regulated by the Legislature: Provided, That no person be eligible or qualified to act as a representative unless he shall have been a citizen of one of the United States three years, and be a resident in the district, or unless he shall have resided in the district three years; and in either case, shall likewise hold in his own right, in fee simple, two hundred acres of land within the same: Provided, also, That a freehold in fifty acres of land in the district, having been a citizen of one of the States, and being resident in the district, or the like freehold and two years' residence in the district, shall be necessary to qualify a man as an elector of a representative.

The representatives thus elected shall serve for

the term of two years; and in case of the death of a representative, or removal from office, the governor shall issue a writ to the county or township for which he was a member to elect another in his stead, to serve for the residue of the term.

The General Assembly, or Legislature, shall consist of the governor, legislative council, and a house of representatives. The legislative council shall consist of five members, to continue in office five years, unless sooner removed by Congress, any three of whom to be a quorum; and the members of the council shall be nominated and appointed in the following manner, to-wit: As soon as representatives shall be elected, the governor shall appoint a time and place for them to meet together, and when met, they shall nominate ten persons, residents in the district, and each possessed of a freehold in five hundred acres of land, and return their names to Congress; five of whom Congress shall appoint and commission to serve as aforesaid; and whenever a vacancy shall happen in the council, by death or removal from office, the house of representatives shall nominate two persons, qualified as aforesaid, for each vacancy, and return their names to Congress; one of whom Congress shall appoint and commission for the residue of the term. And every five years, four months at least before the expiration of the time of service of the members of the council, the said house shall nominate ten persons, qualified as aforesaid, and return their names to Congress; five of whom Congress shall appoint and commission to serve as members of the council five years, unless sooner removed. And the governor, legislative council, and house of representatives, shall have authority to make laws in all cases for the good government of the district, not repugnant to the principles and articles in this ordinance established and declared, and all bills having passed by a majority in the house, and by a majority in the council, shall be referred to the governor for his assent; but no bill or legislative act whatever shall be of any force without his assent. The governor shall have power to convene, prorogue, and dissolve the General Assembly when in his opinion it shall be expedient.

The governor, judges, legislative council, secretary, and such other officers as Congress shall appoint in the district, shall take an oath or affirmation of fidelity and of office, the governor before the President of Congress, and all other officers before the governor. As soon as a Legislature shall be formed in the district, the council and house assemble, in one room, shall have authority, by joint ballot, to elect a delegate to Congress, who shall have a seat in Congress, with a right of debating, but not of voting during this temporary government.

And for extending the fundamental principles of civil and religious liberty, which form the basis whereon these republics, their laws and constitutions, are erected; to fix and establish those principles as the basis of all laws, constitutions, and governments, which forever hereafter shall be formed in the said Territory; to provide, also, for

15

the establishment of States, and permanent government therein, and for their admission to a share in the Federal councils on an equal footing with the original States, at as early periods as may be consistent with the general interest:

It is hereby ordained and declared, by the authority aforesaid, That the following articles shall be considered as articles of compact, between the original States and the people and States in the said Territory, and forever remain unalterable, unless by common consent, to-wit:

Article I. No person, demeaning himself in a peaceable and orderly manner, shall ever be molested on account of his mode of worship or religious sentiments, in the said Territory.

Article II. The inhabitants of the said Territory shall always be entitled to the benefits of the writ of habeas corpus, and of the trial by jury; of a proportionate representation of the people in the Legislature, and of judicial proceedings according to the course of the common law. All persons shall be bailable, unless for capital offenses, where the proof shall be evident or the presumption great. All fines shall be moderate; and no cruel or unusual punishments shall be inflicted. No man shall be deprived of his liberty or property but by the judgment of his peers, or the law of the land; and should the public exigencies make it necessary for the common preservation to take any person's property, or to demand his particular services, full compensation shall be made for the same. And, in the just preservation of rights and property, it is understood and declared that no law ought ever to be made, or have force in the said Territory, that shall, in any manner whatever, interfere with, or affect, private contracts or engagements, bona fide and without fraud, previously formed.

Article III. Religion, morality, and knowledge, being necessary to good government and the happiness of mankind, schools and the means of education shall forever be encouraged. The utmost good faith shall always be observed toward the Indians; their lands and property shall never be taken from them without their consent; and in their property, rights, and liberty they shall never be invaded or disturbed, unless in just and lawful wars authorized by Congress; but laws founded in justice and humanity shall, from time to time, be made for preventing wrongs being done to them, and for preserving peace and friendship with them.

Article IV. The said Territory, and the States which may be formed therein, shall ever remain a part of this confederacy of the United States of America, subject to the Articles of Confederation, and to such alterations therein as shall be constitutionally made; and to all the acts and ordinances of the United States in Congress assembled, conformable thereto. The inhabitants and settlers in the Territory shall be subject to pay a part of the Federal debts, contracted or to be contracted, and a proportional part of the expenses of Government, to be apportioned on them by Congress, according

to the same common rule and measure by which
apportionments thereof shall be made on the
other States; and the taxes for paying their proportion shall be laid and levied by the authority
and direction of Legislatures of the district or districts, or new States, as in the original States,
within the time agreed upon by the United States
in Congress assembled. The Legislatures of those
districts, or new States shall never interfere with
the primary disposal of the soil by the United
States in Congress assembled, nor with any regulations Congress may find necessary for securing the
title in such soil to the bona fide purchasers. No
tax shall be imposed on lands the property of the
United States; and in no case shall non-resident
proprietors be taxed higher than residents. The
navigable waters leading into the Mississippi and
St. Lawrence, and the carrying places between the
same, shall be common highways, and forever free,
as well to the inhabitants of the said Territory as
to the citizens of the United States, and those of
any other States that may be admitted into the
confederacy, without any tax, impost, or duty
therefor.

Article V. There shall be formed in the said
Territory not less than three, nor more than five
States; and the boundaries of the States, as soon
as Virginia shall alter her act of cession, and
consent to the same, shall become fixed and established as follows, to-wit: The western State in
the said territory shall be bounded by the Mississippi, the Ohio, and Wabash Rivers; a direct line

drawn from the Wabash and Post Vincents, due
north, to the territorial line between the United
States and Canada; and by the said territorial
line to the Lake of the Woods and Mississippi. The
middle States shall be bounded by the said direct
line, the Wabash, from Post Vincents to the Ohio,
by the Ohio, by a direct line drawn due north
from the mouth of the Great Miami to the said territorial line, and by the said territorial line. The
eastern State shall be bounded by the last mentioned direct line, the Ohio, Pennsylvania, and
the said territorial line: Provided, however, and it
is further understood and declared, that the boundaries of these three States shall be subject so far
to be altered, that, if Congress shall hereafter find
it expedient, they shall have authority to form one
or two States in that part of the said Territory
which lies north of an east and west line drawn
through the southerly bend or extreme of Lake
Michigan. And whenever any of the said States
shall have sixty thousand free inhabitants therein,
such State shall be admitted, by its delegates, into
the Congress of the United States, on an equal footing with the original States in all respects whatever; and shall be at liberty to form a permanent
Constitution and State government: Provided,
the constitution and government so to be formed
shall be republican, and in conformity to the principles contained in these articles; and, so far as
it can be consistent with the general interest of
the confederacy, such admission shall be allowed
at an earlier period, and when there may be a

less number of free inhabitants in the State than sixty thousand.

Article VI. There shall be neither slavery nor involuntary servitude in the said Territory, otherwise than in the punishment of crimes, whereof the party shall have been duly convicted: Provided always, that any person escaping into the same, from whom labor or service is lawfully claimed in any one of the original States, such fugitive may be lawfully reclaimed, and conveyed to the person claiming his or her labor or service as aforesaid.

Be it ordained by the authority aforesaid, That the resolutions of the 23d of April, 1784, relative to the subject of this ordinance, be, and the same are hereby repealed and declared null and void.

Done by the United States in Congress assembled the thirteenth day of July, in the year of our Lord one thousand seven hundred and eighty-seven, and of their sovereignty and independence the twelfth.

CHARLES THOMPSON, Secretary.

CHAPTER V.

THE CONSTITUTION OF THE UNITED STATES.

SKETCH OF THE ORIGIN OF THE CONSTITUTION.—TEXT
OF THE CONSTITUTION.—TEXT OF AMENDMENTS
TO THE CONSTITUTION.—CHRONOLOGY
OF AMENDMENTS TO THE CON-
STITUTION.

From the time the colonies united, in September, 1774, to obtain their rights under the British crown, until the Articles of Confederation went into effect, March 1, 1781, the government of the Union was only a revolutionary league. The government of the Union under the Articles of Confederation was one step forward in constitutional government. But not a long one, however, for it was so weak, owing to the manner of its formation, that it can hardly be dignified with the name of a national government. It, however, answered a purpose. It demonstrated to the people of the United States that, "the political union of the people of the United States for certain limited purposes, as distinguished from a union of the States of which they are citizens," was an absolute necessity; and that only by a union of the people of all the States, which should combine a portion of their sovereign power in the hands of one directing power, and make them one people, could America ever hope to take a high place among the nations of the world.

The government of the Confederation "introduced to men's minds the great ideas of national power and national sovereignty, as the agencies

that were to work out the difficult results which
no local power could accomplish; and, although
these ideas were at first vague and indefinite, and
made but a slow and difficult progress against
influences and prejudices of a narrower kind, they
were planted in the thoughts of men, to ripen into
maturity and strength in the progress of future
years."[14]

Alexander Hamilton, of New York, early saw
the vital defects of the Confederation; and when
an opportunity was presented he exerted all his
genius and influence to remedy the defects by having a constitution enacted which should be based
on the Declaration that, governments derive "their
just powers from the consent of the governed;
that, whenever any form of government becomes
destructive of these ends, it is the right of the
people to alter or to abolish it, and to institute
a new government, laying its foundation on such
principles, and organizing its powers in such form,
as to them shall seem most likely to effect their
safety and happiness."

The government of the United States, under
the Articles of Confederation, had no power to
make uniform commercial regulations either as
between the States or with foreign governments.
Indeed, it had no power over commerce whatever.
The result was a condition of chaos in the matter
of the trade of the United States. It soon became
apparent that without a uniform system in their

---

[14]Curtis, Const. Hist. of U. S.

commercial regulations there would be no permanent harmony, and trade would languish.

Owing to the trade regulations between Virginia and Maryland, it came about that the Legislature of Virginia, on January 21, 1786, passed a resolution in these words:

"Resolved, That Edmund Randolph, James Madison, Jr., Walter Jones, St. George Tucker, Meriweather Smith, David Ross, William Ronald, and George Mason, Esquires, be appointed commissioners, who, or any five of whom, shall meet such commissioners as may be appointed by the other States in the Union, at a time and place to be agreed on, to take into consideration the trade of the United States; to examine the relative situation and trade of the said States; to consider how far a uniform system in their commercial regulations may be necessary to their common interest and their permanent harmony; and to report to the several States such an act relative to this great object as, when unanimously ratified by them, will enable the United States in Congress assembled effectually to provide for the same; that the said commissioners shall immediately transmit to the several States copies of the preceding resolution, with a circular letter respecting their concurrence therein, and proposing a time and place for the meeting aforesaid."

It was now that the influence of Alexander Hamilton was exerted with all his genius for a better government, and a more perfect union,—for a radical change in the foundation principles of the national government. He succeeded in having the Legislature of his State, New York, appoint commissioners to attend the commercial convention, recommended by Virginia, and he was appointed one of them.

In the circular letter which transmitted the resolution of Virginia recommending the convention to the several States, it was proposed that the convention meet in September, 1786, at Annapolis, Maryland. The convention met at that place, in September of 1786, but when Hamilton arrived he found there the representatives of five States only.[15] It is said that he came with the determination that the convention should lay before the country the whole subject of the condition of the United States, and the want of an efficient national government. But the object of the meeting, as stated in the resolution of the Legislature of Virginia, was only to consider the means of establishing a uniform system of commercial regulations, and not the reform of the existing government of the Union. New Jersey alone, of the five States represented, had empowered her commissioners to consider of "other important matters," besides commercial regulations. Four other States had appointed commissioners, none of whom attended the convention, and the four remaining States had made no appointment at all.

With five States only represented, Hamilton waived his original purpose of a full exposition of the fundamental defects of the Confederation,

---

[15] New York, New Jersey, Pennsylvania, Delaware, and Virginia.

but he did not deem it expedient that the convention should adjourn without proposing some measure that might lead to the necessary reforms. He, therefore, modified his original plan and laid before the convention a report which proposed to the several States the calling of a General Convention, to take into consideration the situation of the United States. This report was agreed to by the Convention.

It declared, among other things, that the regulation of trade could not be effected alone, as the regulating of commerce would so far enter into the general system of the national or federal government that it would require a change in the other parts of the system. That the system of the general government, under the Articles of Confederation, was seriously defective; and that some mode by which these defects could be peaceably supplied was imperatively demanded. A general convention of delegates from the several States, with the power of investigating the defects of the national government, seemed to be the best course to pursue to bring the matter before the Congress, and the country.

It was, indeed, the only method by which Hamilton's object, in its entirety, could be reached in safety. His ultimate object had to be reached by indirect methods or it might fail. The Articles of Confederation had provided that no alteration should be made in any of the Articles, unless agreed to in a Congress of the United States, and confirmed by the legislature of every State.[16] To have left the matter to Congress would have defeated the great reform which Hamilton contemplated—the substitution of an entire different system of national government; for Congress were limited in their power under the Articles. At the same time it was necessary to have the co-operation of the Congress in order to the success of the plan of a convention, that it might not appear to be revolutionary in its character, and for the sake of their influence with the States. Hence the caution observed by Hamilton in his report. It did not suggest a convention to frame a new constitution of national government, but "to devise such further provisions as might appear to be necessary to render the constitution of the federal government adequate to the exigencies of the Union." It proposed, also, that whatever should be agreed on by the Convention should be reported to Congress, and, when agreed to by them, should be ratified by the legislatures of all the States.

Hamilton, however, undoubtedly contemplated more than a revision of the Articles of Confederation by this proposed convention. In 1780 he had analyzed the defects of the Articles, and sketched the outline of a constitution for a strong national government; and, also, suggested the calling of a convention to frame such a system.[17] The idea of such a convention had been entertained, by many persons, before the meeting at Annapolis.

---

[16] See Article XIII.
[17] See his letter to James Duane, written in 1780, "Life of Hamilton," Vol. I, 284-305.

The first public proposal of a continental convention is assigned by Madison to one Pelatiah Webster, who made this suggestion in a pamphlet published in May, 1781. In the summer of 1782 the legislature of New York, under the suggestion of Hamilton, passed resolutions recommending such a convention. On the 1st of April, 1783, Hamilton, in a debate in Congress, expressed his desire to see a general convention take place. In 1784 the measure was a good deal talked of among the members of Congress, and in the winter of 1784-85, Noah Webster, an eminent political writer in Connecticut, suggested "a new system of government, which should act, not on the States, but directly on individuals, and vest in Congress full power to carry its laws into effect." In 1786 the subject was again talked of among members of Congress, before the meeting at Annapolis. But Hamilton's letter to James Duane, in 1780, although not published at the time, was of course earlier than any of these suggestions.[18]

Congress, after much hesitation, approved of the plan of a General Convention, as proposed by the convention of commissioners at Annapolis; and recommended that "on the second Monday in May next, a convention of delegates, who shall have been appointed by the several States, be held at Philadelphia, for the sole and express purpose of revising the Articles of Confederation, and reporting to Congress and the several legislatures such alterations and provisions therein as shall,

---

[18]Curtis, Const. Hist. of the U. S.

when agreed to in Congress and confirmed by the
States, render the Federal Constitution adequate
to the exigencies of government and the preservation of the Union.[19]"

A point was now gained, by this action of Congress, of vast and decisive importance. That the
Congress should give up their right to originate
changes in the system of national government; that
it should sanction a general revision of the Constitution then in force, by an outside body, with
an expression that "experience hath evinced that
there are defects in the present Confederation;"
and that "such a convention appearing to be the
most probable means of establishing in these
States a firm national government,"—were all pre-
liminaries essential to a thorough reformation of
the national government. The time had now come,
however, to establish a constitution of government
on the principles announced in the Declaration of
Independence. For this we are indebted to no
one more than to Alexander Hamilton.

Having thus, briefly, sketched the origin of the
Convention, I proceed now, in as brief a way as
possible, to the doings of that Convention.

All the thirteen States, except Rhode Island,
having selected delegates, through their legislatures—from the body of the people—these delegates met at Philadelphia, on the 14th day of May,
1787,—the place and time fixed by Congress—
fifty-five attending the Convention. George Washington was unanimously chosen as its President;

---

[19]Journals of Cong., Vol. XII, 17, February 21, 1787.

Alexander Hamilton, James Madison, Benjamin Franklin, Gouverneur Morris, Rufus King, Charles Cotesworth Pinckney, James Wilson, Edmund Randolph, Roger Sherman, John Dickinson, Robert Morris, Charles Pinckney, George Mason, and John Rutledge, were among its most distinguished members.

The Convention being now organized the delegates were ready to begin the great task before them. How well they performed that great task the result of their work speaks for itself. Suffice it to say that the Constitution framed by them is the best example of a constitution of government ever devised by man; and will ever remain a monument to their wisdom.

Under the resolution of Congress authorizing the Convention, the only power given its members was, "of revising the Articles of Confederation, and reporting to Congress and the several legislatures such alterations and provisions therein as shall, when agreed to in Congress and confirmed by the States, render the Federal Constitution adequate to the exigencies of government and the preservation of the Union." The first question, then, that came up was, Is it possible to revise the Articles of Confederation so as to "render the Federal Constitution adequate to the exigencies of government and the preservation of the Union?" They answered this in the negative. It would seem, then, that after this answer the Convention had no further duties to perform, except to adjourn. But this they did not do, but proceeded to the formation of an entirely new constitution as a substitute for the Articles of Confederation.

Two questions now arose: What shall the new constitution be? and how shall it be established? The answers to these took time, reflection, argument, concession, compromise, and wise statesmanship, coupled with a large knowledge of the science of government.

The members of the Convention had now launched out on their own responsibility to reform the existing national government; and it would seem that from this time, at least, the Convention became a revolutionary body. They now acted contrary to and against the existing constitution, and outside of the powers granted them by the Congress; they assumed to act in the name of "We, the people." They assumed the power, in the name of the people of the United States, to form "a more perfect union, establish justice, insure domestic tranquillity, provide for the common defense, promote the general welfare, and secure the blessings of liberty to themselves and their posterity." They assumed, however, the power simply of framing a constitution, which they hoped would secure these great objects to the people of the United States, and of submitting it to the people for final action. It would seem that they acted on the theory that it did not make any difference who drew up the Constitution so that it was submitted to the people of the United States for their ratification. In this they were right. Of course the act was revolutionary, but that was the only way left under existing circumstances, of founding a government based on "the consent of the governed."

Hence the members of that Convention assumed to act as the representatives of the people of the United States in order to form a constitution of government for the Union, which should be submitted to them for their adoption or rejection, in their sovereign capacity as the holders of all political power. In other words, the people of the United States were recognized, by these proceedings, as the American state—the original sovereign power of the land; whereas before this they were not so recognized, at least, in national governmental matters, for the Articles of Confederation were made by sovereign States in their corporate capacities—the people, as such, were ignored.

With this assumption of power, as the basis of their acts, the delegates proceeded to the formation of the Constitution. The first question now that arose was, What are the necessary constituent powers of a free government? It was soon determined that a well balanced republican government should consist of three general departments, namely, the legislative, the executive, and the judicial. With this as the foundation of the new Constitution the Convention began its labors of constructing the Constitution. Herein consisted the great work of the Convention.

As it was designed to be an efficient national government, one with powers "adequate to the exigencies of government and the preservation of the Union," it was necessary to carefully consider

16

what powers should be given it to carry out these great objects, and not infringe on the necessary powers of the States for local government. These were matters of great moment to be determined with the utmost precision; for on this adjustment of powers, as between the National and the State governments, depended the harmonious working of the whole system of government, then being devised.

With what far-seeing statesmanship did these men give to one the powers necessary to carry out national objects; to the other those powers necessary only for the promotion of local affairs. The national government was made so that it would be over all—its constitution, treaties, and laws, were to be the supreme law of the land. All other constitutions and laws were made subordinate to these.

Finally, after four months of great anxiety and hard labor, the Constitution was agreed on and signed by thirty-nine members of the Convention, September 17, 1787, and was now ready for submission to the people of the United States for their adoption or rejection as they might deem best. And that there might be no mistake that the new Constitution was to be the people's constitution, it was provided in the Constitution, in addition to the preamble, that "the ratification of the Conventions of nine States shall be sufficient for the establishment of this Constitution between the States so ratifying the same."

It has been related, as a tradition, that when Washington was about to sign the Constitution, he rose from his seat, and, holding the pen in his hand, after a short pause, said: "Should the States reject this excellent Constitution, the probability is that an opportunity will never again offer to cancel another in peace—the next will be drawn in blood."

The Constitution having been adopted by the Convention was then transmitted to Congress, with the recommendation that it should "be submitted to a convention of delegates chosen in each State by the people thereof, under a recommendation of its legislature, for their assent and ratification." Congress thereupon adopted a resolution transmitting it to the State legislatures, "in order to be submitted to a convention of delegates chosen in each State by the people thereof, in conformity to the resolves of the Convention made and provided in that case."[20]

In accordance with these resolves of the Convention and the Congress, conventions were called in all the States and delegates elected to attend the same.

After the Constitution left the hands of the Convention which framed it, it passed through a severe ordeal. As soon as it was known what had been done in the Convention at Philadelphia—the sessions of the Convention were secret—a powerful opposition rose against the Constitution in some of the States which threatened its rejection, and called forth all the energies and influence of its ablest friends—Washington, Hamilton, Madison,

[20]Passed September 28, 1787. Journals XII, 149-166.

Franklin, James Wilson, and Charles Cotesworth
Pinckney being of the number who ably promoted
its adoption by the people.

But to no other agency are we more indebted
for its adoption, than to the efforts put forth by
Madison and Hamilton with John Jay, who used
their great talents and influence in the way of argument, addressed to the people, in their celebrated essays called "The Federalist." It was from
Hamilton's essays, says an eminent writer, that
the Federalist chiefly derived the weight and the
power which carried conviction to a large body of
intelligent men in all parts of the Union. Out of
the total number of essays contained in the Federalist (eighty-five), Hamilton, it is said, wrote fifty-
one, and assisted in writing some of the others. So
long as the Constitution shall exist, these essays
will be resorted to as the most important sources
of contemporaneous interpretation which the history of the country affords.

The Constitution, indeed, needed powerful advocates; for it met with powerful opposition in
some of the States when it came before the Conventions of the people for ratification. The Confederation had been made by the States in their
corporate capacities. The States were jealous of
their rights; and now to be ignored, as such, in
the making of a new constitution of government,
as a substitute for the Confederation, aroused all
the energies of those who believed in a confederation of the States, rather than in a strong national
government made by the people.

Patrick Henry, the great orator of Virginia, used all his influence against the adoption of the Constitution in the Convention of the people of that State. He asked, "Who authorized them (the framers of the Constitution) to speak the language of 'We, the people,' instead of 'We, the States'?" "States," said he, "are the characteristic and the soul of a confederation. If the States be not the agents of this compact, it must be one great consolidated national government of the people of all the States." George Mason, another powerful opponent of the new Constitution, said in the same Convention: "Whether the Constitution be good or bad, the present clause clearly discovers that it is a national government, and no longer a confederation."

However, in 1788 the people of eleven States had ratified the new Constitution. The other two —Rhode Island and North Carolina—did not adopt it until early in 1790. The government went into operation, however, under the Constitution,— by an act of Congress,—on March 4th, 1789; although, owing to delays, Washington, the first President, was not inaugurated until April 30th of that year.

It may be truly said, I think, that the making of the Constitution, by the people of the United States, and putting the government into operation under it, was as much a revolution as was the revolution by which our independence was gained of Great Britain; peaceable, it is true, but nevertheless revolution. For, as has been said before in this chapter, the Articles of Confederation—the existing law when this new Constitution was made and went into effect—prescribed that no alteration should be made in the Articles except by the Congress and the approval by the legislature of every State. This provision was undoubtedly violated in the making of the Constitution. The people of the United States, under the Confederation, took it into their own hands to make a constitution of government conformable to their will,—majority will,—and by adopting the Constitution, and organizing and putting into operation a government under it, overturned the Confederate constitution and government made by the States.

We may well say that, under the combination of circumstances, the result was but little short of a miracle; and, as Kent has well said, "the peaceable adoption of this government, under all the circumstances which attended it, presented the case of an effort of deliberation, combined with a spirit of amity and of mutual concession, which was without example. It must be a source of just pride, and of the most grateful recollection, to every American, who reflects seriously on the difficulty of the experiment, the manner in which it was conducted, the felicity of its issue, and the fate of similar trials in other nations of the earth."

Constitution of the United States of America.

The following is an exact copy, in capitals, orthography, text, and punctuation, of the Constitution of the United States of America, as proposed and adopted by the Convention held at Philadelphia, September 17, 1787, and afterwards ratified by the people of the several original States:

We the People of the United States, in Order to form a more perfect Union, establish Justice, insure domestic Tranquility, provide for the common defence, promote the general Welfare, and secure the Blessings of Liberty to ourselves and our Posterity, do ordain and establish this Constitution for the United States of America.

ARTICLE. I.

Section. 1. All legislative Powers herein granted shall be vested in a Congress[21] of the United States, which shall consist of a Senate and House of Representatives.

Section. 2. The House of Representatives shall be composed of Members chosen every second Year by the People of the several States, and the Electors in each State shall have the Qualifications requisite for Electors of the most numerous Branch of the State Legislature.

No Person shall be a Representative who shall not have attained to the Age of twenty five Years, and been seven Years a Citizen of the United States, and who shall not, when elected, be an Inhabitant of that State in which he shall be chosen.

Representatives and direct Taxes shall be apportioned among the several States which may be included within this Union, according to their re-

[21]Congress meets in regular session on the first Monday in December of each year; the session closes, by custom, at midnight on the third of the following March. Each Congress exists two years.

spective Numbers, [which shall be determined by adding to the whole Number of free Persons, including those bound to Service for a Term of Years, and excluding Indians not taxed, three fifths of all other Persons[22]]. The actual Enumeration shall be made within three Years after the first Meeting of the Congress of the United States, and within every subsequent Term of ten Years, in such Manner as they shall by Law direct. The Number of Representatives shall not exceed one for every thirty Thousand, but each State shall have at Least one Representative; and until such enumeration shall be made, the State of New Hampshire shall be entitled to chuse three, Massachusetts eight, Rhode-Island and Providence Plantations one, Connecticut five, New-York six, New Jersey four, Pennsylvania eight, Delaware one, Maryland six, Virginia ten, North Carolina five, South Carolina five, and Georgia three.[22*]

When vacancies happen in the Representation from any State, the Executive Authority thereof shall issue Writs of Election to fill such Vacancies.

The House of Representatives shall chuse their Speaker and other Officers; and shall have the sole Power of Impeachment.

Section. 3. The Senate of the United States shall be composed of two Senators from each

---

[22]"Persons," meaning slaves. The portion within brackets no longer in force. See Amendments XIII. and XIV. to the Constitution.

[22*]At present (1896) one Representative is sent to Congress for every 173,901 persons.

State, chosen by the Legislature thereof, for six
Years; and each Senator shall have one Vote.

Immediately after they shall be assembled in
Consequence of the first Election, they shall be
divided as equally as may be into three Classes.
The Seats of the Senators of the first Class shall
be vacated at the Expiration of the second Year,
of the second Class at the Expiration of the fourth
Year, and of the third Class at the Expiration of
the sixth Year, so that one third may be chosen
every second Year; and if Vacancies happen by
Resignation, or otherwise, during the Recess of
the Legislature of any State, the Executive thereof
may make temporary Appointments until the next
Meeting of the Legislature, which shall then fill
such Vacancies.

No Person shall be a Senator who shall not
have attained to the Age of thirty Years, and been
nine Years a Citizen of the United States, and who
shall not, when elected, be an Inhabitant of that
State for which he shall be chosen.

The Vice President of the United States shall
be President of the Senate, but shall have no
Vote, unless they be equally divided.

The Senate shall chuse their other Officers, and
also a President pro tempore, in the Absence of the
Vice President, or when he shall exercise the Office of President of the United States.

The Senate shall have the sole Power to try all
Impeachments. When sitting for that Purpose,
they shall be on Oath or Affirmation. When the
President of the United States is tried, the Chief

Justice shall preside: And no Person shall be convicted without the Concurrence of two thirds of the Members present.

Judgment in Cases of Impeachment shall not extend further than to removal from Office, and disqualification to hold and enjoy any Office of honor, Trust or Profit under the United States: but the Party convicted shall nevertheless be liable and subject to Indictment, Trial, Judgment and Punishment, according to Law.

Section. 4. The Times, Places and Manner of holding Elections for Senators and Representatives, shall be prescribed in each State by the Legislature thereof; but the Congress may at any time by Law make or alter such Regulations, except as to the Places of chusing Senators.

The Congress shall assemble at least once in every Year, and such Meeting shall be on the first Monday in December, unless they shall by Law appoint a different Day.

Section. 5. Each House shall be the Judge of the Elections, Returns and Qualifications of its own Members, and a Majority of each shall constitute a Quorum to do Business; but a smaller Number may adjourn from day to day, and may be authorized to compel the Attendance of absent Members, in such Manner, and under such Penalties as each House may provide.

Each House may determine the Rules of its Proceedings, punish its Members for disorderly Behaviour, and, with the Concurrence of two thirds, expel a Member.

Each House shall keep a Journal of its Proceedings, and from time to time publish the same, excepting such Parts as may in their Judgment require Secrecy; and the Yeas and Nays of the Members of either House on any question shall, at the Desire of one fifth of those Present, be entered on the Journal.

Neither House, during the Session of Congress, shall, without the Consent of the other, adjourn for more than three days, nor to any other Place than that in which the two Houses shall be sitting.

Section. 6.   The Senators and Representatives shall receive a Compensation[23] for their Services, to be ascertained by Law, and paid out of the Treasury of the United States. They shall in all Cases, except Treason, Felony and Breach of the Peace, be privileged from Arrest during their Attendance at the Session of their respective Houses, and in going to and returning from the same; and for any Speech or Debate in either House, they shall not be questioned in any other Place.

No Senator or Representative shall, during the Time for which he was elected, be appointed to any civil Office under the Authority of the United States, which shall have been created, or the Emoluments whereof shall have been encreased during such time; and no Person holding any Office under the United States, shall be a Member of either House during his Continuance in Office.

Section. 7.   All Bills for raising Revenue shall

---

[23]Fixed by Congress at $5,000 a year, with twenty cents for every mile necessarily travelled in coming to and returning from the Capital.

originate in the House of Representatives; but the
Senate may propose or concur with Amendments
as on other Bills.

Every Bill which shall have passed the House
of Representatives and the Senate, shall, before
it become a Law, be presented to the President of
the United States; If he approve he shall sign it,
but if not he shall return it, with his Objections
to that House in which it shall have originated,
who shall enter the Objections at large on their
Journal, and proceed to reconsider it. If after such
Reconsideration two thirds of that House shall
agree to pass the Bill, it shall be sent, together with
the Objections, to the other House, by which it
shall likewise be reconsidered, and if approved by
two thirds of that House, it shall become a Law.
But in all such Cases the Votes of both Houses
shall be determined by Yeas and Nays, and the
Names of the Persons voting for and against the
Bill shall be entered on the Journal of each House
respectively. If any Bill shall not be returned
by the President within ten Days (Sundays excepted) after it shall have been presented to him,
the Same shall be a law, in like Manner as if he
had signed it, unless the Congress by their Adjournment prevent its Return, in which Case it
shall not be a Law.

Every Order, Resolution, or Vote to which the
Concurrence of the Senate and House of Representatives may be necessary (except on a question
of Adjournment) shall be presented to the President of the United States; and before the Same

shall take Effect, shall be approved by him, or being disapproved by him, shall be repassed by two thirds of the Senate and House of Representatives, according to the Rules and Limitations prescribed in the Case of a Bill.

Section. 8. The Congress shall have Power

To lay and collect Taxes, Duties, Imposts and Excises, to pay the Debts and provide for the common Defence and general Welfare of the United States; but all Duties, Imposts and Excises shall be uniform throughout the United States;

To borrow Money on the credit of the United States;

To regulate Commerce with foreign Nations, and among the several States, and with the Indian Tribes;

To establish an uniform Rule of Naturalization, and uniform Laws on the subject of Bankruptcies throughout the United States;

To coin Money, regulate the Value thereof, and of foreign Coin, and fix the Standard of Weights and Measures;

To provide for the Punishment of counterfeiting the Securities and current Coin of the United States;

To establish Post Offices and post Roads;

To promote the Progress of Science and useful Arts, by securing for limited Times to Authors and Inventors the exclusive Right to their respective Writings and Discoveries;

To constitute Tribunals inferior to the supreme Court;

To define and punish Piracies and Felonies committed on the high Seas, and Offences against the Law of Nations;

To declare War, grant Letters of Marque and Reprisal, and make Rules concerning Captures on Land and Water;

To raise and support Armies, but no Appropriation of Money to that Use shall be for a longer Term than two Years;

To provide and maintain a Navy;

To make Rules for the Government and Regulation of the land and naval Forces;

To provide for calling forth the Militia to execute the Laws of the Union, suppress Insurrections and repel Invasions;

To provide for organizing, arming, and disciplining, the Militia, and for governing such Part of them as may be employed in the Service of the United States, reserving to the States respectively, the Appointment of the Officers, and the Authority of training the Militia according to the discipline prescribed by Congress;

To exercise exclusive Legislation in all Cases whatsoever, over such District (not exceeding ten Miles square) as may, by Cession of particular States, and the Acceptance of Congress, become the Seat of the Government of the United States, and to exercise like Authority over all Places purchased by the Consent of the Legislature of the State in which the Same shall be, for the Erection of Forts, Magazines, Arsenals, dock-Yards, and other needful Buildings;—And

To make all Laws which shall be necessary and proper for carrying into Execution the foregoing Powers, and all other Powers vested by this Constitution in the Government of the United States, or in any Department or Officer thereof.

Section. 9. The Migration or Importation of such Persons as any of the States now existing shall think proper to admit, shall not be prohibited by the Congress prior to the Year one thousand eight hundred and eight, but a Tax or duty may be imposed on such Importation, not exceeding ten dollars for each Person.[24]

The Privilege of the Writ of Habeas Corpus shall not be suspended, unless when in Cases of Rebellion or Invasion the public Safety may require it.

No Bill of Attainder or ex post facto Law shall be passed.

No Capitation, or other direct, Tax shall be laid, unless in Proportion to the Census or Enumeration hereinbefore directed to be taken.

No Tax or Duty shall be laid on Articles exported from any State.

No Preference shall be given by any Regulation of Commerce or Revenue to the Ports of one State over those of another: nor shall Vessels bound to, or from, one State, be obliged to enter, clear, or pay Duties in another.

No Money shall be drawn from the Treasury, but in Consequence of Appropriations made by

[24]"Person," meaning slave; referring to the foreign slave-trade then being carried on. This slave-trade prohibited by Congress in 1808.

Law; and a regular Statement and Account of the Receipts and Expenditures of all public Money shall be published from time to time.

No Title of Nobility shall be granted by the United States: And no Person holding any Office of Profit or Trust under them, shall, without the Consent of the Congress, accept of any Present, Emolument, Office, or Title, of any kind whatever, from any King, Prince, or foreign State.

Section. 10. No State shall enter into any Treaty, Alliance, or Confederation; grant Letters of Marque and Reprisal; coin Money; emit Bills of Credit; make any Thing but gold and silver Coin a Tender in Payment of Debts; pass any Bill of Attainder, ex post facto Law, or Law impairing the Obligation of Contracts, or grant any Title of Nobility.

No State shall, without the Consent of the Congress, lay any Imposts or Duties on Imports or Exports, except what may be absolutely necessary for executing it's inspection Laws: and the net Produce of all Duties and Imposts, laid by any State on Imports or Exports, shall be for the Use of the Treasury of the United States; and all such Laws shall be subject to the Revision and Controul of the Congress.

No State shall, without the Consent of Congress, lay any Duty of Tonnage, keep Troops, or Ships of War in time of Peace, enter into any Agreement or Compact with another State, or with a foreign Power, or engage in War, unless actually invaded, or in such imminent Danger as will not admit of delay.

ARTICLE. II.

Section. 1. The executive Power shall be vested in a President of the United States of America. He shall hold his Office during the Term of four Years, and, together with the Vice President, chosen for the same Term, be elected, as follows

Each State shall appoint, in such Manner as the Legislature thereof may direct, a Number of Electors, equal to the whole Number of Senators and Representatives to which the State may be entitled in the Congress: but no Senator or Representative, or Person holding an Office of Trust or Profit under the United States, shall be appointed an Elector.

*[The Electors shall meet in their respective States, and vote by Ballot for two Persons, of whom one at least shall not be an Inhabitant of the same State with themselves. And they shall make a List of all the Persons voted for, and of the Number of Votes for each; which List they shall sign and certify, and transmit sealed to the Seat of the Government of the United States, directed to the President of the Senate. The President of the Senate shall, in the Presence of the Senate and House of Representatives, open all the Certificates, and the Votes shall then be counted. The Person having the greatest Number of Votes shall be the President, if such Number be a Majority of the whole Number of Electors appointed; and if there

---

*The paragraph within brackets rendered null and void by the XIIth Amendment.

17

be more than one who have such Majority, and
have an equal Number of Votes, then the House of
Representatives shall immediately chuse by Ballot
one of them for President; and if no Person have
a Majority, then from the five highest on the List
the said House shall in like Manner chuse the
President. But in chusing the President, the Votes
shall be taken by States, the Representation from
each State having one Vote; A quorum for this
Purpose shall consist of a Member or Members
from two thirds of the States, and a Majority of all
the States shall be necessary to a Choice. In every
Case, after the Choice of the President, the Person
having the greatest Number of Votes of the Electors shall be the Vice President. But if there
should remain two or more who have equal Votes,
the Senate shall chuse from them by Ballot the
Vice President.]

The Congress may determine the Time of
chusing the Electors, and the Day on which they
shall give their Votes; which Day shall be the
same throughout the United States.[25]

No Person except a natural born Citizen, or a
Citizen of the United States, at the time of the
Adoption of this Constitution, shall be eligible to
the Office of President; neither shall any Person
be eligible to that Office who shall not have attained to the Age of thirty five Years, and been

---

[25]The electors are chosen on the Tuesday following the first Mon-
day in November next before the expiration of a presidential term.
They vote (by Act of Congress of February 3, 1887) on the second
Monday in January following for President and Vice-President.
The votes are counted, and declared in Congress on the second
Wednesday of the next February.

fourteen Years a Resident within the United States.

In Case of the Removal of the President from Office, or of his Death, Resignation, or Inability to discharge the Powers and Duties of the said Office, the Same shall devolve on the Vice President, and the Congress may by Law provide for the Case of Removal, Death, Resignation or Inability, both of the President and Vice President, declaring what Officer shall then act as President, and such Officer shall act accordingly, until the Disability be removed, or a President shall be elected.

The President shall, at stated Times, receive for his Services, a Compensation,[26] which shall neither be encreased nor diminished during the Period for which he shall have been elected, and he shall not receive within that Period any other Emolument from the United States, or any of them.

Before he enter on the Execution of his Office, he shall take the following Oath or Affirmation:—

"I do solemnly swear (or affirm) that I will faithfully execute the Office of President of the United States, and will to the best of my Ability, preserve, protect and defend the Constitution of the United States."

Section. 2. The President shall be Commander in Chief of the Army and Navy of the United States, and of the Militia of the several States, when called into the actual Service of the United

---

[26]The President now receives $50,000 a year; the Vice-President $8,000. Previous to 1872, the President received but $25,000 a year.

States; he may require the Opinion, in writing, of the principal Officer in each of the executive Departments, upon any Subject relating to the Duties of their respective Offices, and he shall have Power to grant Reprieves and Pardons for Offences against the United States, except in Cases of Impeachment.

He shall have Power, by and with the Advice and Consent of the Senate, to make Treaties, provided two thirds of the Senators present concur; and he shall nominate, and by and with the Advice and Consent of the Senate, shall appoint Ambassadors, other public Ministers and Consuls, Judges of the supreme Court, and all other Officers of the United States, whose Appointments are not herein otherwise provided for, and which shall be established by Law: but the Congress may by Law vest the Appointment of such inferior Officers, as they think proper, in the President alone, in the Courts of Law, or in the Heads of Departments.

The President shall have Power to fill up all Vacancies that may happen during the Recess of the Senate, by granting Commissions which shall expire at the End of their next Session.

Section. 3. He shall from time to time give to the Congress Information of the State of the Union, and recommend to their Consideration such Measures as he shall judge necessary and expedient; he may, on extraordinary Occasions, convene both Houses, or either of them, and in Case of Disagreement between them, with Respect to the Time of Adjournment, he may adjourn them to such Time as he shall think proper; he shall receive Ambassadors and other public Ministers; he shall take Care that the Laws be faithfully executed, and shall Commission all the officers of the United States.

Section. 4. The President, Vice President and all civil Officers of the United States, shall be removed from Office on Impeachment for, and Conviction of, Treason, Bribery, or other high Crimes and Misdemeanors.

ARTICLE. III.

Section. 1. The judicial Power of the United States, shall be vested in one supreme Court, and in such inferior Courts as the Congress may from time to time ordain and establish. The Judges, both of the supreme and inferior Courts, shall hold their Offices during good Behaviour, and shall, at stated Times, receive for their Services, a Compensation, which shall not be diminished during their Continuance in Office.

Section. 2. The judicial Power shall extend to all Cases, in Law and Equity, arising under this Constitution, the Laws of the United States, and Treaties made, or which shall be made, under their Authority;—to all Cases affecting Ambassadors, other public Ministers and Consuls;—to all Cases of admiralty and maritime Jurisdiction;—to Controversies to which the United States shall be a Party;—to Controversies between two or more States;—between a State and Citizens of another

State;—between Citizens of different States,—between Citizens of the same State claiming Lands under Grants of different States, and between a State, or the Citizens thereof, and foreign States, Citizens or Subjects.

In all Cases affecting Ambassadors, other public Ministers and Consuls, and those in which a State shall be Party, the supreme Court shall have original Jurisdiction. In all the other Cases before mentioned, the supreme Court shall have appellate Jurisdiction, both as to Law and Fact, with such Exceptions, and under such Regulations as the Congress shall make.

The Trial of all Crimes, except in Cases of Impeachment, shall be by Jury; and such Trial shall be held in the State where the said Crimes shall have been committed; but when not committed within any State, the Trial shall be at such Place or Places as the Congress may by Law have directed.

Section. 3. Treason against the United States, shall consist only in levying War against them, or in adhering to their Enemies, giving them Aid and Comfort. No person shall be convicted of Treason unless on the Testimony of two Witnesses to the same overt Act, or on Confession in open Court.

The Congress shall have Power to declare the Punishment of Treason, but no Attainder of Treason shall work Corruption of Blood, or Forfeiture except during the Life of the Person attainted.

ARTICLE. IV.

Section. 1. Full Faith and Credit shall be given in each State to the public Acts, Records, and judicial Proceedings of every other State. And the Congress may by general Laws prescribe the Manner in which such Acts, Records and Proceedings shall be proved, and the Effect thereof.

Section. 2. The Citizens of each State shall be entitled to all Privileges and Immunities of Citizens in the several States.

A Person charged in any State with Treason, Felony, or other Crime, who shall flee from Justice, and be found in another State, shall on Demand of the executive Authority of the State from which he fled, be delivered up, to be removed to the State having Jurisdiction of the Crime.

No Person[27] held to Service or Labour in one State, under the Laws thereof, escaping into another, shall, in Consequence of any Law or Regulation therein, be discharged from such Service or Labour, but shall be delivered up on Claim of the Party to whom such Service or Labour may be due.

Section. 3. New States may be admitted by the Congress into this Union; but no new State shall be formed or erected within the Jurisdiction of any other State; nor any State be formed by the Junction of two or more States, or Parts of States, without the Consent of the Legislatures of the States concerned as well as of the Congress.

[27]"Person" here means slave. This clause of Section 2, Article IV, has no force now, as slavery was abolished by Amendment XIII. to the Constitution.

The Congress shall have Power to dispose of and make all needful Rules and Regulations respecting the Territory or other Property belonging to the United States; and nothing in this Constitution shall be so construed as to Prejudice any Claims of the United States, or of any particular State.

Section. 4. The United States shall guarantee to every State in this Union a Republican Form of Government, and shall protect each of them against Invasion; and on Application of the Legislature, or of the Executive (when the Legislature cannot be convened) against domestic Violence.

ARTICLE. V.

The Congress, whenever two thirds of both Houses shall deem it necessary, shall propose Amendments to this Constitution, or, on the Application of the Legislatures of two thirds of the several States, shall call a Convention for proposing Amendments, which, in either Case, shall be valid to all Intents and Purposes, as Part of this Constitution, when ratified by the Legislatures of three fourths of the several States, or by Conventions in three fourths thereof, as the one or the other Mode of Ratification may be proposed by the Congress: Provided that no Amendment which may be made prior to the Year One thousand eight hundred and eight shall in any Manner affect the first and fourth Clauses in the Ninth Section of the first Article; and that no State, without its

Consent, shall be deprived of it's equal Suffrage in the Senate.

ARTICLE. VI.

All Debts contracted and Engagements entered into, before the Adoption of this Constitution, shall be as valid against the United States under this Constitution, as under the Confederation.

This Constitution, and the Laws of the United States which shall be made in Pursuance thereof; and all Treaties made, or which shall be made, under the Authority of the United States, shall be the supreme Law of the Land; and the Judges in every State shall be bound thereby, any Thing in the Constitution or Laws of any State to the Con- trary notwithstanding.

The Senators and Representatives before men- tioned, and the Members of the several State Legis- latures, and all executive and judicial Officers, both of the United States and of the several States, shall be bound by Oath or Affirmation, to sup-- port this Constitution; but no religious Test shall ever be required as a qualification to any Office or public Trust under the United States.

ARTICLE. VII.

The Ratification of the Conventions of nine States, shall be sufficient for the Establishment of this Constitution between the States so ratifying the Same.

Done in Convention by the Unanimous Consent of the States present the Seventeenth Day of September in the Year of our Lord one thousand seven hundred and Eighty seven and of the Independence of the United States of America the Twelfth **In Witness** whereof We have hereunto subscribed our Names.

GO. WASHINGTON—Presidt.
and Deputy from Virginia.

NEW HAMPSHIRE.

JOHN LANGDON.   NICHOLAS GILMAN.

MASSACHUSETTS.

NATHANIEL GORHAM.   RUFUS KING.

CONNECTICUT.

WM. SAM'L JOHNSON.   ROGER SHERMAN.

NEW YORK.

ALEXANDER HAMILTON.

NEW JERSEY.

WIL: LIVINGSTON.   WM. PATERSON.
DAVID BREARLEY.   JONA: DAYTON.

PENNSYLVANIA.

B. FRANKLIN.   THOS. FITZ SIMONS.
THOMAS MIFFLIN.   JARED INGERSOLL.
ROBT. MORRIS.   JAMES WILSON.
GEO. CLYMER.   GOUV MORRIS.

DELAWARE.

GEO: READ.   RICHARD BASSETT.
GUNNING BEDFORD, JUN.   JACO: BROOM.
JOHN DICKINSON.

MARYLAND.

JAMES McHENRY.   DANL. CARROLL.
DAN OF ST. THOS. JENIFER.

VIRGINIA.

JOHN BLAIR.   JAMES MADISON, JR.

SOUTH CAROLINA.

CHARLES C. PINCKNEY.   J RUTLEDGE.
CHARLES PINCKNEY.   PIERCE BUTLER.

NORTH CAROLINA.

WM. BLOUNT.   HU WILLIAMSON.
RICHD. DOBBS SPAIGHT.

GEORGIA.

WILLIAM FEW.   ABR. BALDWIN.
Attest: WILLIAM JACKSON, Secretary.

ARTICLES IN ADDITION TO, AND AMENDMENT OF, THE
CONSTITUTION OF THE UNITED STATES
OF AMERICA.

Proposed by Congress and Ratified by the Legislatures of the
several States, pursuant to the Fifth Article of
the Original Constitution.

ARTICLE I.

Congress shall make no law respecting an establishment of religion, or prohibiting the free exercise thereof; or abridging the freedom of speech, or of the press; or the right of the people peaceably to assemble, and to petition the government for a redress of grievances.

ARTICLE II.

A well regulated militia being necessary to the security of a free state, the right of the people to keep and bear arms shall not be infringed.

ARTICLE III.

No soldier shall, in time of peace, be quartered in any house without the consent of the owner: nor in time of war, but in a manner to be prescribed by law.

ARTICLE IV.

The right of the people to be secure in their persons, houses, papers, and effects, against un-

reasonable searches and seizures, shall not be violated; and no warrants shall issue, but upon prob-
ble cause, supported by oath or affirmation, and
particularly describing the place to be searched,
and the persons or things to be seized.

ARTICLE V.

No person shall be held to answer for a capital,
or otherwise infamous crime, unless on a present-
ment or indictment of a grand jury, except in cases
arising in the land or naval forces, or in the militia,
when in actual service, in time of war or public
danger; nor shall any person be subject, for the
same offense, to be twice put in jeopardy of life or
limb; nor shall be compelled, in any criminal case,
to be a witness against himself; nor be deprived of
life, liberty, or property, without due process of
law; nor shall private property be taken for public
use without just compensation.

ARTICLE VI.

In all criminal prosecutions, the accused shall
enjoy the right to a speedy and public trial, by an
impartial jury of the State and district wherein
the crime shall have been committed, which district shall have been previously ascertained by
law, and to be informed of the nature and cause
of the accusation; to be confronted with the witnesses against him; to have compulsory process
for obtaining witnesses in his favor; and to have
the assistance of counsel for his defense.

ARTICLE VII.

In suits at common law, where the value in controversy shall exceed twenty dollars, the right of trial by jury shall be preserved; and no fact, tried by a jury, shall be otherwise re-examined in any court of the United States, than according to the rules of the common law.

ARTICLE VIII.

Excessive bail shall not be required, nor excessive fines imposed, nor cruel and unusual punishments inflicted.

ARTICLE IX.

The enumeration in the Constitution, of certain rights, shall not be construed to deny or disparage others retained by the people.

ARTICLE X.

The powers not delegated to the United States by the Constitution, nor prohibited by it to the States, are reserved to the States respectively or to the people.

ARTICLE XI.

The judicial power of the United States shall not be construed to extend to any suit in law or equity, commenced or prosecuted against one of the United States by citizens of another State, or by citizens or subjects of any foreign State.

ARTICLE XII.

The electors shall meet in their respective States, and vote by ballot for President and Vice-President, one of whom, at least, shall not be an inhabitant of the same State with themselves; they shall name in their ballots the person voted for as President, and in distinct ballots the person voted for as Vice-President; and they shall make distinct lists of all persons voted for as President, and of all persons voted for as Vice-President, and of the number of votes for each, which lists they shall sign and certify, and transmit sealed to the seat of the government of the United States, directed to the President of the Senate; the President of the Senate shall, in the presence of the Senate and House of Representatives, open all the certificates, and the votes shall then be counted; the person having the greatest number of votes for President shall be the President, if such number be a majority of the whole number of electors appointed; and if no person have such majority, then from the persons having the highest numbers, not exceeding three, on the list of those voted for as President, the House of Representatives shall choose immediately, by ballot, the President. But in choosing the President, the votes shall be taken by States, the representation from each State having one vote; a quorum for this purpose shall consist of a member or members from two-thirds of the States, and a majority of all the States shall be necessary to a choice. And if the House of Representatives

shall not choose a President, whenever the right
of choice shall devolve upon them, before the
fourth day of March next following, then the Vice-
President shall act as President, as in the case of
the death or other constitutional disability of the
President.

The person having the greatest number of
votes as Vice-President shall be the Vice-President, if such number be a majority of the whole
number of electors appointed; and if no person
have a majority, then from the two highest numbers on the list, the Senate shall choose the Vice-
President; a quorum for that purpose shall consist
of two-thirds of the whole number of Senators, and
a majority of the whole number shall be necessary
to a choice.

But no person constitutionally ineligible to
the office of President shall be eligible to that of
Vice-President of the United States.

ARTICLE XIII.

Sec. 1. Neither slavery nor involuntary servitude, except as a punishment for crime, whereof
the party shall have been duly convicted, shall exist within the United States, or any place subject
to their jurisdiction.

Sec. 2. Congress shall have power to enforce
this article by appropriate legislation.

ARTICLE XIV.

Sec. 1. All persons born or naturalized in the

United States, and subject to the jurisdiction
thereof, are citizens of the United States and of the
State wherein they reside. No State shall make
or enforce any law which shall abridge the privileges or immunities of citizens of the United
States; nor shall any State deprive any person of
life, liberty, or property, without due process of
law, nor deny to any person within its jurisdiction
the equal protection of the laws.

Sec. 2. Representatives shall be apportioned
among the several States, according to their respective numbers, counting the whole number of
persons in each State, excluding Indians not
taxed. But when the right to vote at any election
for the choice of electors for President and Vice-
President of the United States, representatives in
Congress, the executive and judicial officers of a
State, or the members of the legislature thereof,
is denied to any of the male inhabitants of such
State, being twenty-one years of age, and citizens
of the United States, or in any way abridged, except for participation in rebellion or other crime,
the basis of representation therein shall be reduced
in the proportion which the number of male
citizens shall bear to the whole number of male
citizens twenty-one years of age in such State.

Sec. 3. No person shall be a Senator or Representative in Congress, or elector of President and
Vice-President, or hold any office, civil or military,
under the United States, or under any State, who,
having previously taken an oath, as a member of

Congress, or as an officer of the United States, or as a member of any State Legislature, or as an executive or judicial officer of any State, to support the Constitution of the United States, shall have engaged in insurrection or rebellion against the same, or given aid or comfort to the enemies thereof. But Congress may, by a vote of two-thirds of each House, remove such disability.

Sec. 4. The validity of the public debt of the United States, authorized by law, including debts incurred for payment of pensions and bounties for services in suppressing insurrection or rebellion, shall not be questioned. But neither the United States nor any State shall assume or pay any debt or obligation incurred in aid of insurrection or rebellion against the United States, or any claim for the loss or emancipation of any slave; but all such debts, obligations, and claims shall be held illegal and void.

Sec. 5. The Congress shall have power to enforce, by appropriate legislation, the provisions of this article.

ARTICLE XV.

Sec. 1. The right of citizens of the United States to vote shall not be denied or abridged by the United States or by any State on account of race, color, or previous condition of servitude.

Sec. 2. The Congress shall have power to enforce this article by appropriate legislation.

NOTE.

The Emancipation Proclamation, of President Lincoln, freed the slaves in the States and parts of States in rebellion, on the 1st day of January, 1863. That proclamation was supplemented by the XIII amendment to the Constitution, which freed all the slaves in the United States. The XIV amendment made all the freedmen (negroes) "citizens" of the United States; and the object of the XV amendment was to give them the right to "vote."

CHRONOLOGY OF AMENDMENTS TO THE CONSTITUTION OF THE UNITED STATES.

The first ten Articles of Amendments were proposed by Congress in 1789, at their first session; they were ratified by the legislatures of three-fourths of the several States, and became a part of the Constitution December 15, 1791.

The eleventh Article was proposed by Congress in 1794. President Adams declared in his message, January 8, 1798, that it had received the ratification of the constitutional number of States, and was therefore a part of the fundamental law of the land.

The twelfth Article of Amendments was proposed by Congress at their session in 1803, and was duly ratified during the following year, and became a part of the Constitution of the United States.

The thirteenth Article of Amendments was proposed at the second session of the thirty-eighth Congress, passing the Senate in 1864, and the House in 1865. William II. Seward, then Secre tary of State, officially announced to the country, December 18, 1865, that it had been ratified by three-fourths of the States, and was therefore a part of the supreme law of the land.

The fourteenth Article of Amendments was proposed by Congress in 1866. William H. Seward, Secretary of State, announced July 28, 1868, that it had been ratified by the legislatures of the re- quisite number of States, and had, therefore, be- come a part of the Constitution.

The fifteenth Article of Amendments was pro- posed by Congress in 1869. Hamilton Fish, then Secretary of State, announced March 30, 1870, that it had been ratified by the requisite number of States, and was, therefore, a part of the Constitu- tion of the United States.

CHAPTER VI.

INDEX AND ANALYSIS OF THE CONSTITUTION.

A

* A stands for AMENDMENT in this chapter.

E

F

H

Q

R

INDEX OF PERSONS.

295